THE ANANSE STROKE

The 4-Letter West African Alphabet for Revival

Bridging Ancestral Knowledge and Artificial Intelligence for Human Upliftment

K. OGYAKRA

Copyright© 2025 by K. OGYAKRA. All rights reserved.

No part of this book may be reproduced, stored in a retrieval system, or transmitted in any form or by any means, electronic, mechanical, photocopying, recording, or otherwise, without the prior written permission of the publisher, except in the case of brief quotations used in critical articles or reviews.

Printed in the United States of America Publisher: Self-Published by K.

OGYAKRA Cover Design: K. OGYAKRA

This is a work of Linguistics, African Spirituality, and Technology.

TABLE OF CONTENTS

FOUNDATIONS 1
  Prologue- Sound as Spirit, Language as Temple, Europe's Disruption 1
  The Skeleton- Language as Body, Organic Vs Polished Pumpkin 5
  Proof Of Language- Evidence Across Tongues 7
  English: Sounds vs. Letters 7
  Twi: Tone, Word-Building, Distributed Meaning 8
  Scholars' note (Panini & Minimal pairs) 9
  Summary: Toward Four Letter 10
  The Collapse Into 4-From 26 To 22 To 4 11

DEDICATION & GUIDANCE 16
  Dedication (Grandparent, Parents, Mentors) 16
  VISION 18
  Foreword (Stephen Pinkard) 19
  How To Use This Book & Basic Rules 21
  Note To the Reader 23
  Introduction 24

CORE SYSTEM 29
  The Ananse Stroke- The Heart of the System 29
  Ananse Alphabet 36
  Bilabials 37
  Alveolars 44
  VELARS 52
  VOWEL 61

Introduction & Mnemonic	61
Stroke Unfolding (Head + Members)	63
Flow Of Stroke	64
Ancestral/Culture View (Queen, King, Priest, People)	65
Practice & Q&A (With Spider Encouragement)	67
Test Your Knowledge	68
Test Your Knowledge	69
Integration	69
A REMINDER	70
Word of Encouragement	71
How It All Ties Together-Lip, Ridge, Throat, Breath as Web	72
Test Your Knowledge	74
Writing practice	77
Sound Weaver-Title and Quantum Bridge	81
BEYOND WRITING: QUANTUM & PRIVACY	**82**
Ananse & Quantum Computing- Shells as Quantum States	82
Ananse Keyword - Interface Of The Future	85
Meta & AI	88
Private System - Personal Cipher, Shared Bridge	91
COMPARATIVE LINGUISTICS & CRITIQUE	**93**
Minimalism, Hangeul, and Chomsky on the Ananse Script	93
Dual Path- Traditional Vs Ananse Simplicity	96
Differentiation In Ananse- Homograpgh, Homophones, Context	100
French Connection- Elegance, Excess, And Hidden Hypocrisy	104
Personalities Of Language-Soldier, Courtier, King, Seer, Etc.	109

Language Acquisition- Acquisition Vs Memorization 114

Talking Drums-Tone as Law, African Science, Colonial Theft 116

Tone, Diacritic-Placement + Curve = Sound + Sound 119

The Ananse stroke with E 125

Ntumpan- Great Drum as Voice of Kinship 127

MASTERY 128

Exam-Ananse Writing System (20 Question + Answer Key) 128

Postscript Beyond the Basics 132

From Language to Spirit - Writing as Shrine and Memory 133

Twi Language Depth - Ka & Ba, Continuity & Spirit 134

Manifesto 1- A Cry for Grounding 136

Manifesto 2 - A Call for Healing 139

Manifesto 3 - True Worship Vs Neglect 142

Respect Overdue - Shrines and Sacred Spaces 143

Final Exam- Comprehensive Review 145

Afterword - Exodus, Unity and Spirit Restored 153

REFERENCE AND END MATTER 154

Definition And Disclaimer 154

Glossary Of Linguistic Terms 158

References 160

IPA 164

FOUNDATIONS

Prologue- Sound as Spirit, Language as Temple, Europe's Disruption

We all once saw a divine force in everything—in the movement of the stars and the silence between them, in the smallest particles and the vastest spaces. What some call God Almighty: never absent, always present, unseen yet holding all things within itself.

Every culture spoke to that force through sound. Chant, drum, prayer, and song were not just expressions—they were bridges to the unseen. Sound was spirit, alive, a force of creation.

Europe had its monks and psalms, its Druids and Bards. Africa had its drums, its tones, its sacred names and invocations. Indigenous peoples across the earth had chants, breath, and vibration as their temples. It was once universal: to speak was to release power.

If sound was once spirit, then language was its temple. Every culture designed a system to hold what the voice carried. We all built languages that guarded the breath, but a shift happened.

Slowly, Europe turned sound into utility. Letters became contracts, laws, and ledgers. The living breath was flattened into marks on paper. Sound was stored, but its spirit was forgotten.

Africa and other Indigenous worlds kept a stronger attachment to sound as spirit. Their languages still carried tone and rhythm as law, their words still rooted in living breath.

Yet even here, the divine knowledge was devalued. Like the Abusua and other sacred inheritances, it was treated harshly, stripped of its inner force, and left as surface performance. We still speak tone, we still chant, but we no longer live its power.

The road we take is always shaping us, shaping how we think, how we live, even the health of our bodies and the condition of our societies. Sound was once a force of peace and unity, but now it often clashes and divides.

Still, even if much of this feels like it was designed long before us, we are not without choice. There are always roads before us. We stand here today because of the power to change. Without it, what would life be? What would remain?

When I look back, I see why West Africa stands where it does today. The Sahara was more than sand; it was a wall. It cut us off from the currents of philosophy, science, and writing flowing through North and Northeast Africa. Once we shared in the cradle of civilization, but after what I call a reset, we were separated from the wider exchange of humanity. In that isolation, we slowed. Then Europe arrived by sea. Their ships carried not only goods but a frequency, the rhythm of another age. We felt it. We knew we were behind in the tools of that moment, and that is what Europe exploited. Trade began again, not across the desert but through their ships. And what went out from us was not only gold. We gave lives, labor, and spirit sons and daughters carried away. What came back were things we already knew in substance, only packaged nicely for trade: cloth, liquor, trinkets. And there was something entirely new - the gun. With the gun came a deeper wound: it turned brother against brother, kingdom against kingdom, multiplying bloodshed and feeding the very trade that weakened us. What had once been disputes became wars, and what had once been wars became devastation. From the very moment their ships reached our shores, we began to bend. We bent ourselves to fit their design. We gave our children foreign names. We allowed even our spiritual concepts to be changed, exchanging our rhythms of the unseen for theirs. We traded memory for convenience and mistook the visitor for the savior. We must not forget the Almoravids, the crossings of the Sahara, and how long the push and pull of history shaped us before the ships ever came. What happened was not only Europe's hand, but also our forgetting, our failure to carry sound into its higher purpose. And so here we are in 2025, still in the struggle. Still caught between memory and forgetting, between spirit and utility. This book arises from that place not to repeat the bending, but to restore what was left behind. It is about a writing system, born from Africa's ground yet shaped for all tongues, so that sound may once again be seen in its true form: alive, and carrying us forward.

Historians' View

Before we step directly into language, let us pause. Historians themselves agree that what we are living through is no ordinary moment. They see the pace of change, the weight of culture, and the shifts that shape us all. To understand why language matters so much now, we must first see the larger picture they describe. Historians may not call it a single reset, but they agree on what our ancestors always knew: humanity moves in shifts. Sometimes slow, sometimes fast. Right now, the pace has quickened to breakneck speed, technology, culture, and institutions racing ahead of our bodies, memories, and traditions. Some name this the Anthropocene, an age where human activity has become the dominant force on the planet. Others call it cultural acceleration, where knowledge, systems, and tools evolve faster than our ability to ground them. Whatever the name, it marks a turning point in the story of humanity.

But here is the truth: Africans carry a heavier weight into this acceleration. While others race forward, we continue to push against centuries of interruption, erasure, and sabotage. Our languages, once living temples of sound, are pushed to the margins. The new global operating system runs on English, French, Spanish, and code. It asks us to morph away from ourselves just to participate. It preserves Western memory while flattening our own. This is why the struggle continues in 2025. Advancement is real, but it is not equal. Cultures are advancing, yes, but for Africans, far more must be overcome before our voices, our tones, and our systems can stand fully in the future. And yet, even within this, there are those who fight to close the gap.

Humanitarians, philosophers, and thinkers across the world labor to restore dignity where it was denied, to build bridges between cultures rather than erase them. Their work is slow, but it is a reminder that the road ahead is not fixed; it is still being written.

And if the road ahead is still being written, then we must ask: with what are we writing it? Nothing shapes the path of humanity more quietly, yet more powerfully, than language. The letters we use, the sounds we keep or lose, all of it decides how the story continues.

The Skeleton- Language as Body, Organic Vs Polished Pumpkin

Imagining it, I see language like a body. The skeleton holds up whatever it's fed. West African languages are like the organic pumpkin in the market, smaller maybe, but natural, balanced, grown in its own soil. English is like the big polished one sprayed to shine, made to look like more, and so people choose it. It feeds a lot —yes, technology, speed, comfort —but it also starves a lot, especially the spirituality of people to actually know themselves. It leaves many moving in a trance, chasing a negative individuality, the same divide-and-conquer pattern carrying on. People think they have free will, but free will under what context, under what frequency? This generation is fascinated by what English feeds them: instant information, bright screens, and new tools. It is, in many ways, their time. But what are we trading for all of this? What are we actually feeding them? Had West Africa been allowed to usher its culture into this age, would the world be as it is today, modernizing ourselves on our own terms? Other nations, like China, were given that chance; they suffered oppression, too, but they modernized themselves in this age. Africa was not given that chance. We are behind in age. When the ships first arrived, we knew we were behind, and even today, We still feel that spirit of being behind. That is why so many African leaders abandon their own native tongues to speak foreign ones — reaching for the shiny pumpkin, even as our own languages are starved and suppressed. The proof is here: the condition of the language shows the condition of the world. English leads, and the world reflects it — restless, packaged, fractured. West African languages stayed pure longer, but being cut off, they were starved; now they are being pressured to trade away their contentedness. That is the same truth, seen from another angle.

And I wonder, what if the organic pumpkin had been polished by its own people, not sprayed with chemicals, not packaged by outsiders, but given an organic way to shine? A beautification that stayed true to its soil. Had we been allowed to hold our languages, our culture, our relics without oppression, we could have stood brighter. Not only in body but in mind. Not only free from physical chains but free from mental ones. We could have contributed even more to the upliftment of humanity. Leading the world... Instead, our relics have been hidden, our contributions suppressed, our tongues silenced. Even today, there are efforts to rewrite our past, to say our greatness was not ours. And now, in this age of artificial intelligence, a new threat rises. These systems are being programmed; biases are already showing. If they are built on the same erasure, they will continue erasing our languages, our history, our image. We cannot take this lightly. What is it about us that demands such suppression? What power do we hold that requires such lengths to keep it down? This is the question the world refuses to face, and the question we must face ourselves. With that said, let us now move on to look inside the languages themselves, where spirit and utility reveal their skeletons.

Proof Of Language- Evidence Across Tongues

Proof In the Languages Themselves

The contrast between spirit and utility can be seen most clearly inside the languages themselves

English: Sounds vs. Letters

English writes with 26 letters, but it actually speaks with about 40 distinct sounds (scholars call these phonemes; I will call them sounds).

We know this because of minimal pairs, words that differ by only one sound but change meaning:

- Pat vs. bat → /p/ vs. /b/
- Thin vs. then → /θ/ vs. /ð/
- Sip vs. ship → /s/ vs. /ʃ/

These pairs prove that English has more sounds than letters to represent them

The problem grows larger with vowels. English vowels are not just single sounds; many are diphthong vowel sounds sliding into another inside the same syllable:

- /aɪ/ as in price
- /aʊ/ as in house
- /ɔɪ/ as in boy

Because of this, English has more than a dozen vowel sounds, far beyond what five letters (A, E, I, O, U) can cover.

To bridge this gap, English uses digraphs, two letters for one sound:

- sh → /ʃ/ (ship)
- th → /θ/ (thin) or /ð/ (this)
- ch → /tʃ/ (chip)
- ph → /f/ (phone)
- Plus vowel pairs like ea in seat, oo in book or food, ou in house, ai in rain, oy in boy.

This patchwork is why English spelling feels irregular. Its letters and sounds don't match neatly. Scholars call this a deep orthography, meaning the writing hides history as much as it reveals sound.

Add to this the long history of borrowing. English absorbed words from Latin, French, Norse, and beyond. Instead of simplifying, it carried them all, often keeping foreign spellings while twisting the sounds. That is why words like through, though, tough, and cough look alike but sound completely different.

And on top of this, English often loads one word with many meanings. Scholars call this polysemy. Run can mean to move quickly, to manage a company, to flow like water, or to operate a machine. These overlaps come from centuries of borrowing, stretching, and reshaping words.

So English works in two ways:

- Too few letters for too many sounds, irregular spelling.
- Too many meanings in one word, you must master context to understand it

Twi: Tone, Word-Building, Distributed Meaning

African Languages (Twi as Example)

By contrast, African languages hold sound closer to their spiritual essence.

- Tone: Pitch itself separates meaning. In Twi, **Kɔ** means "go" while **Kɔ** (with high tone) can mean "fight." The same letters, but the tone makes a new word. Tone keeps the word alive.
- Word-building (morphology): Roots expand into families of related words. For example, the root ka in Twi can mean "to speak." From it we get **Nkɔmka** (to prophesy, literally "to speak dreams") and kasa (speech, language). The root remains, and meaning grows like branches from a trunk.
- Distributed meaning: Instead of overloading one word with 20 meanings like English (run), Twi spreads meaning across tone and form.

In practice:

- English is simple on the outside (26 letters), but forces you to master context inside.
- African languages like Twi are harder to master at first (tone and structure demand discipline), but once inside, they are clearer, more precise, and closer to the sound of the spirit.

Scholars' note (Panini & Minimal pairs)

Linguists use minimal pairs as a scientific way of measuring sound systems. In fact, this method has been a cornerstone of Indian linguistic tradition for centuries. The scholars who preserved Sanskrit grammar, such as **Pāṇini**, broke language down with astonishing precision - not by multiplying letters endlessly, but by carefully defining contrasts between sounds.

This is why India became central in modern linguistics: they showed how minimal pairs can map the full system of a language. To use the same principle today, whether for English, Twi, or Ananse, is to stand in that same scholarly stream.

Summary: Toward Four Letter

Summary: proof in the languages

This is the proof inside the languages themselves: English overloaded with irregularity and context, Africa carrying clarity through tone and root. Scholars confirm the principles, and even India's long tradition shows how minimal pair analysis can reduce complexity to order.

From here, the question is not whether it can be done; the question is how. And that is why in the next part of this prologue, I show how we arrive at four letters, four shells that hold the full system of sound.

The Collapse Into 4-From 26 To 22 To 4

The Collapse Into 4

Note to the Reader

The word collapse in this book does not mean fainting, falling, or breaking apart. Here, collapse means something higher: a field of possibilities focusing into clarity, many states narrowing into one expression, potential becoming order.

From 26 ➜ 22 ➜ 20 Removing Overlap

We begin with the 26 letters of English. In Akan, several of these letters carry no unique sounds because their values are already represented elsewhere. Removing these overlaps takes us from 26 to 22. The omitted letters are: **c, j, q, v, x, z.c** ➜covered by k ("cat") or s ("city") j ➜ represented by gy (as in gyina) q ➜ represented by kw (as in Kwaku) v ➜ by f (as in fie) x represented by ks (as in "box") z ➜ represented by s These letters are redundant. They duplicate what other letters already do. Removing them reduces the alphabet from 26 ➜ 22. Next, for universality and simplicity, we align the system with the five core vowels common to both English and many global languages: A, E, I, O, and U. The Akan language uses seven vowels, but two of these (ɛ and ɔ) are specific to Akan phonology and are therefore not used in this system. Removing them refines the set from 22 to 20 usable sounds. This is the first stage of collapse: stripping away what is unnecessary to reveal what is essential.

Two Types of Redundancy

- Alphabet Overlap: Removing letters whose sounds are already represented (as shown above).

- Source Collapse: Recognizing that many letters are born from the same part of the mouth.

Instead of treating them as separate, we recognize their shared origin: M, N, G, and A as the heads of families. This reduces 20 → 4 shells.

Beyond Raw Memorization

Most alphabets train through raw appearance: one sound, one letter, memorized without question. The Ananse System initiates differently: Know the shell family. Follow the stroke... Placement + curve sound + tone. This is not passive recall. It is active guidance. The stroke becomes an agent of the mind, forcing it to move, choose, and clarify.

The Power of Association

This collapse teaches association: In the material world, one tree trunk, many branches. In the abstract world, love, joy, and compassion all come from the same root. The shells teach the same truth: one root, many expressions.

Superposition and Collapse

Quantum physics teaches that particles exist in a superposition of many states at once until observation collapses them into clarity. Life mirrors this law. In the matrix of daily experience, countless possibilities surround us. What we focus on becomes real. The Ananse Script works the same way: The four shells are

- Superposition.
- The stroke is observed.
- Placement and
- Curves are the rules of focus.

Where alphabets demand passive memory, Ananse demands active collapse of meaning. Architecture and conscious retrieval skills are essential for keeping pace with technology.

Levels of the Mind Shades of Consciousness

1) Surface Memory: recall of shapes.

2) Categorization: grouping by families.

3) Guidance by Law: following placement.

4) Compartmentalization: building mental files.

5) Insight: grasping one root, many expressions.

6) Shades of Consciousness: moving from appearance to depth-surface, middle, root; up, straight, down.

The Gift of Four Letters

From 26 scattered letters to 20 focused sounds to **4 living shells.** Not reduction, but transformation: a law that clarifies thought, awakens association, and trains the mind to see patterns instead of fragments.

Bridge to dedication

Before we go further, step with me for a moment. The laws of shells and strokes are here, but behind them is a life. The Dedication that follows is a light-a glimpse of my upbringing, the hands and voices that shaped me, and the soil from which this work grew. It is memory and continuity-threaded from Ancestors to this very page. Turn now, and see where it begins.

Shaped me, and the soil from which this work grew. It is memory, gratitude, and continuity—a thread from my Ancestors to this very page. Turn now, and see where it all begins.

Ancestral Invocation

Come through the mist... I see you now. I feel you now.

From silence... from code... from time unbound...

You were here and still are.

You are the past... the future...

and the pulse of the present - positioned within all.

You know me. You have chosen me.

You hear the sound of my voice, the sound you have always known.

And I thank you... for helping me realize you are ever-present.

Out of silence... and within all things...

Your presence moves, guiding me still.

I walk with you, and you walk with me always.

DEDICATION & GUIDANCE

Dedication (Grandparent, Parents, Mentors)

This work is dedicated to my Grandparents and Parents, the foundation of all I am. Their lives were lessons written not in ink, but in love, patience, and presence. May these words not only honor them but remind every reader of the quiet inheritance carried within their own families.

To My Grandmother Rahda (Rada) Govinda

She filled every day with proverbs, and her words were jewels: "Learning is better than silver and gold. Even in a divided land, cut off from inheritance, she chose love. Her wisdom showed me that wealth fades, but love endures as the only inheritance worth keeping. Perhaps you, too, remember a proverb or saying passed down a line of wisdom that still guides your steps today.

To My Grandmother Helga Doreen Smith

She carried the story of the turtle and the heir, though the heir was faster; he was distracted. The turtle steadily, faithfully stayed on course and reached the end. So she taught me patience. As a single parent, she walked with quiet strength, never rushing, never giving up. Her dedication marked me forever. Maybe you also had someone who showed you that progress is not about speed, but about faithfulness to the path.

To My Grandfathers

Though I hardly spent time with them, I remain grateful for the paths they walked before me. Their strength and choices shaped the family I was born into, and their lives

gave me the opportunity to stand where I stand today. Even at a distance, their presence was a foundation. Perhaps you, too, carry gratitude for ancestors you hardly knew yet whose footsteps made your own journey possible.

To My Mother, Sandra Browne

She gave me one word: contented. She used it often when I was a child, shaping me into humility. To be contented is to be grounded, to find peace even when little rests in your hands. From her, I learned that gratitude is the richest food for the soul. What single word has shaped you? What lesson from a parent or guardian still nourishes your spirit?

To My Father, Sheridan Braithwaite

Reserved and silent, he taught me that presence is enough, and that dignity often speaks louder than words. Perhaps in your life, too, there was someone who spoke more by silence than by speech.

May these dedications invite you, reader, to pause and remember your own roots, the proverbs of your Grandparents, the patience of your elders, the quiet dignity of your Parents, or the guidance of a mentor, for it is gratitude that makes inheritance rich, and memory that turns family into a foundation. And as their lessons grounded me, so too must we ground ourselves as a people, for the inheritance of script and spirit is not only mine, but ours.

VISION

At first, the path may seem daunting, as new ways often do. But this work is born to restore what Africa was denied: its writing, its clarity, its inheritance, and to inspire beyond Africa alone.

It calls on humanitarians and dreamers everywhere to uplift all people, to see the earth not as overcrowded but as abundant, and to make room for wonders still to come.

This is a vision of restoration and expansion, a vessel to carry memory forward, and to prepare space for futures yet unseen.

Foreword (Stephen Pinkard)

Training Awareness of What Is Usually Unconscious

As you can see for yourself, this is not a book to skim and leave behind. one step leading into another, one stroke. It draws you in differently, unfolding into a pattern.

In Kemet, it was said that voice and sign are not separate but measures of the same truth: one unseen, one seen. This script continues that law.

Some of what you read here, you may already have seen in the Prologue. That is not a mistake but a method. The author explained to me that the repetitions you encounter are deliberate. Rhythm itself is part of the training. What may feel redundant at first is in fact conditioning -fixing the rhythm into your mind so that when you arrive at the shells and the stroke, you are already moving by their law.

The Ananse Script is not about recalling what you already know. In other alphabets, you say, "I need a Y" and summon it from memory. Here you do something different. You begin with the shell and **create the value by law** stroke, placement, and family. The sound does not arrive because you remembered it; it arrives because you performed the rule.

This does not slow the act of writing. It does not change the speed of summoning. What it does is add **layers of awareness** to what is usually unconscious.

Speed is not lost; depth is gained.

Categorization, compartmentalization, retrieval - these are no longer abstract terms; they are motions you make, choices you embody. The unseen field of possibilities is narrowed into clarity each time you move the stroke into place.

The author repeats, and will repeat again, not to waste your time, but to shape your attention. The stroke must become second nature, the collapse must become reflex. This is how you pass from reading into seeing, and from seeing into communion.

And remember: writing is the first discipline, not the last. The clearer your perception, the less you will need marks. The generation to come may speak mind to mind, spirit to spirit, and the Ananse Script will have been their training ground.

The Ananse Script begins as letters. It matures as law. It points toward communion.

And now, before you place your hand on the shells or follow the stroke, **step with me into the rhythm ahead.** What follows is not theory, but method guidance to steady your steps, so the path of the Ananse Script opens clear before you.

→*Stephen Pinkard, in conversation with the author*

How To Use This Book & Basic Rules

How To Use This Book the Simple Way

1. Do not look for ABC.

What you already know of sounds will guide you, but here the alphabet is not chased as 26 letters. It is refined. You subtract the excess and keep what carries meaning. The stroke is not memory; it is law: each mark produces the sound.

2. Think of it as a 3-step ladder.

There is one ladder, built of three steps: top, middle, and root. Each family uses this same ladder. The leader is the ladder itself, the law of placement. The family members stand on its steps in succession. Placement is key.

3. Families and Succession.

There are four families. Each one reveals its members on the 3-step ladder, head to last, step by step. Like Russian dolls, one opens to reveal the next until the family is complete. Family is key. Succession is key.

4. Practice writing.

Do not only read, write. Use the mnemonics in this book to remember the order of succession in each family. Put them on the page and test yourself. With steady effort, within a few days, the rhythm will settle and the families will feel natural.

5. Feel before you read.

Do not rush to symbols. Touch your lips, tap your tongue, breathe out. The body already knows sound; the script only shows what you have always carried.

6. The Four Shells.

Scholars call them bilabial, alveolar, velar, and vowel words that sound heavy. In truth, they are simple: lips, ridge, throat, and open air. The names are foreign, but the sounds are yours.

7. Do not memorize, recognize.

This is not cramming. It is rhythm. See the family, follow the ladder, let the pattern reveal itself. Recognition is memory shaped by law.

8. Learn to associate.

Every principle shows up in different places. The way a sound is placed is like how AI chooses meaning from context, the way a joke works only when timed right, or the way you put on your shoes in their proper order. Different fields, same truth: context and placement. The script plants the idea to think across the board, carrying one principle into another, and in this way, it deepens your sense of context — how each piece belongs to the whole.

9. Pay attention.

When you test yourself, do not think of scores. Think of awareness. Ask: Which ladder am I on? Which step is this family member on? Who is the head? Who is the last? How many members belong here? Placement, family, and succession, this attention is what makes the knowledge stick until the script becomes second nature.

Note To the Reader

Full definitions and disclaimers, including why some sounds in this system differ from the International Phonetic Alphabet (IPA), and why certain principles (such as digraphs) are not included, are kept at the **back of this book.**

Check there if you need details.

WITHOUT FURTHER DELAY, LET'S BEGIN.

Introduction

You just read in How to Use This Book that each family can be thought of as standing on a ladder with three steps. Before we ascend that ladder, I place before you another comparison: the Rubik's Cube set beside the Ananse keyboard.

Cube + Ananse Comparison

The Rubik's Cube begins with six colors. When scrambled, its small squares look scattered and confusing until you learn the pattern that restores them.

Traditional alphabets behave the same way: letters scatter into fragments, and endless rules are needed to hold them together.

The Ananse Script takes the opposite approach. Imagine the cube with only four colors each color a family of sounds. Here the scattering only happens when sounds form words. Even then, the families remain visible: bilabial, alveolar, velar, and vowel.

So while the cube hides order beneath a scramble, the Ananse Script shows order through families. The shells make the pattern visible.

Below you see them side by side: the Cube, a puzzle of hidden order, and the Ananse keyboard, a sketch of future clarity. One teaches how to recognize patterns; the other shows how omission sharpens meaning.

Both teaches pattern recognition and spacial logic

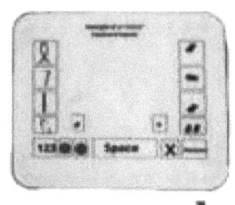

Keyboard concept Explaination later on.

App in progress

Ladder example using the bilabials

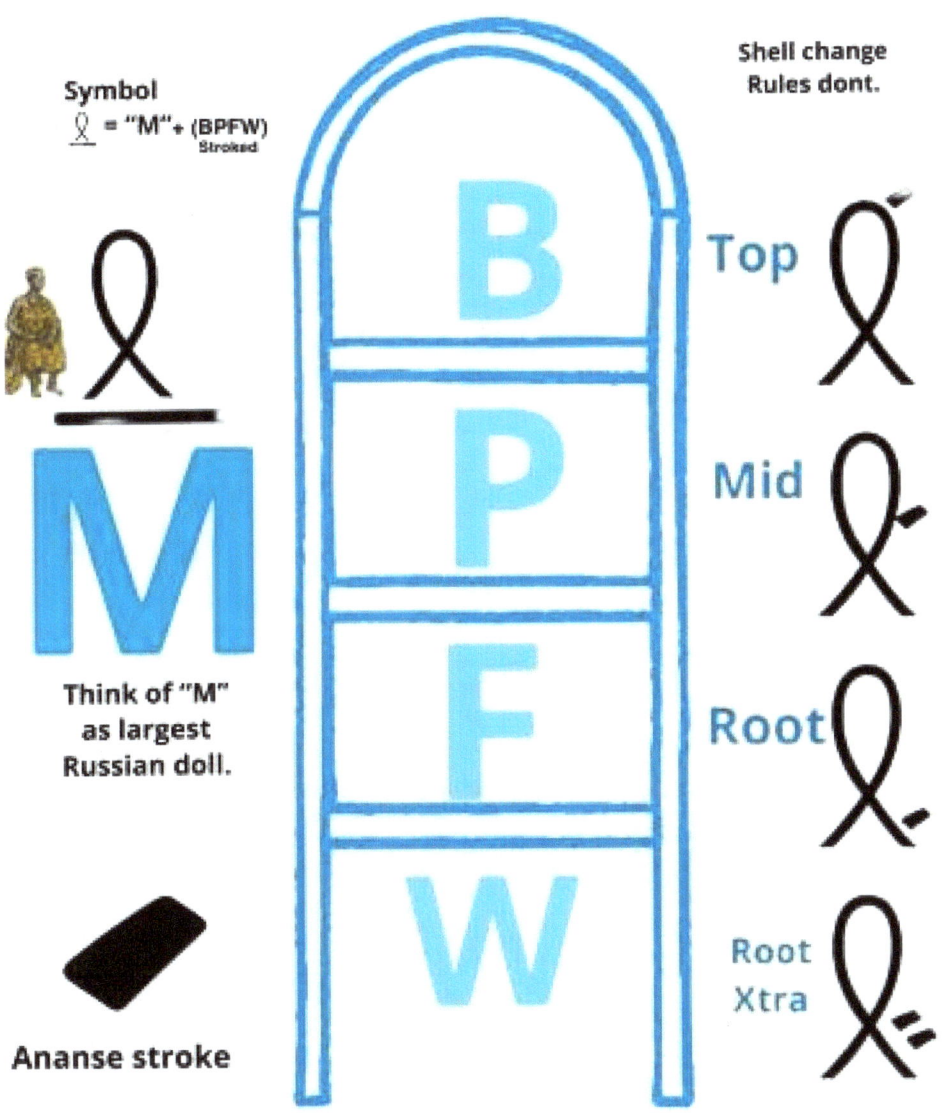

Same shell from the head "M",
top, root "W". Use mnemonic to decipher succession of sounds
Stroke only 3 places. Numbers to remember 4 and 3.

But ideas alone are not enough, writing lives in the body. To see how this works, we need to feel it for ourselves.

Try This Out

Say these words aloud and notice where each sound begins inside your mouth. Each family has its own starting point:

Lip Sounds (Bilabials – M, B, P) man, map, meat, moon, mother, mine, baby, bed, book. Notice: The lips press together first – the gate of sound.

Ridge Sounds (Alveolars N, D, T, L) name, net, note, door, date, top, take, tall, land, lot. Notice: The tongue taps the ridge just behind the teeth where order and rhythm begin.

Throat-Back Sounds (Velars G, K, H): go, game, gold, get, good, give, gone, king, keep, kick, hug, hope. Notice: The back of the tongue lifts, and the sound comes from deeper in the throat.

Open Breath Sounds (Vowels A, E, I, O, U) a, e, i, o, u. Notice: The mouth opens wide and lets the breath flow freely, the sounds of open air.

Note on the shells: Each shell marks a family. When you see the shell, think of the group of sounds that share the same place in your body: lips, tongue, throat, or breath.

You just spoke the words. Pause for a moment and notice what happened. The sounds weren't random; you felt where they rose from, how they settled, and how they gathered in families before spilling into language. That feeling is your first glimpse of order at work.

By the way, you may have noticed I mentioned a keyboard for this writing system. I know I dropped that on you quickly. Think of it as a sketch, a working diagram with only the most minimal characters for greater efficiency. It's not the final form the real magic is still unfolding, with an app already in the making. I wanted you to see that even with a few keys, a whole world can be opened.

And now we come to the thread that ties it all together, the **Ananse Stroke.** It isn't just another mark. It is the weaver's line: the covenant that binds families, directs tone, and keeps balance even as words scatter. This is the heart of the writing system.

CORE SYSTEM

The Ananse Stroke- The Heart of the System

Ananse (The Storyteller) The Heart of the Writing System

Ananse, the spider of Akan folklore, is the storyteller and strategist. With one thread, he spins a whole web: fragile to the eye, yet strong enough to catch and connect the world. That is why the stroke - one line, holding families and tones together carries his name.

The Ananse Stroke is the heart of this writing system. The shells provide structure, but the stroke makes them alive. It is both simple and abstract: a mark so plain it seems empty, yet it carries sound, family, and melody at once.

Across Africa, tone was always central to speech but difficult to capture in writing. Scholars working with borrowed letters, Arabic or Latin, tried to add dots, slashes, and accents to mark tones. Others left tone unmarked entirely, trusting context to guide the reader. And often, context did enough. But not always. A single shift in tone could turn a word into something else entirely, leaving ambiguity where clarity was needed.

The Ananse Script answers this with elegance. It does not depend on extra marks above borrowed letters. It does not abandon tone to context. Instead, the stroke itself carries the role. Whether plain, rising, or falling, the line alone is enough.

This is Ananse's wisdom: what looks like a thread is in fact a world. What looks like a stroke is in fact a system. Without it, the shells remain silent. With it, they speak.

Woven across books

Inspire by google images

HOW THE STROKE WORKS

We've met Ananse, the storyteller, the weaver of webs, the heart of this writing system. Now let's see how his stroke actually works. The stroke carries two layers of power:

1. Placement The stroke begins from one of three positions: Top, Middle, or Root. This is how families are organized by where the sound begins in the mouth (lips, tongue, throat, or breath). Placement tells us where the vibration is born.

2. Alteration Once placed, the stroke may remain flat, curve upward, or curve downward. Flat carries the mid tone. Upward carries the high tone. Downward carries the low tone. Alteration tells us how the vibration moves. So, the stroke does two jobs at once: its position shows the family, and its curve carries the tone. To deepen this system, we link it with the Abusua not because the stroke comes from the Abusua, but because the Abusua reveals Africa's deeper way of organizing life through family and clan. By drawing these links, readers can see that our spiritual and cultural domain has always been about order, balance, and covenant, and not the scattered vibration following the Western way.

Symbolic Parallels of the Shells

Bilabial (Tjet —The Queen Mother)

- The lips, the gate of speech and nourishment.
- Symbolic parallel: The Tjet knot of Kemet, representing protection and life-force.

Alveolar (Scepter — The King)

- The tongue at the ridge, staff of authority and order.
- Symbolic parallel: The scepter, bearer of truth and kingly power.

Velar (Obelisk — The Priest)

- The throat, voice of deep resonance.
- Symbolic parallel: The obelisk, rising to join earth and sky, linking human and divine.

Vowel/Open Breath (Sankofa-inspired — The People)

- The breath itself, free and unbound.
- Symbolic parallel: Sankofa calling us back to what was lost, teaching remembrance and return.

The Abusua

The Akan word Abusua can be broken down as:

Abu — family, group, or clan

Sua — portion, part, or branch

Together, Abusua means **"family lineage" or "clan";** belonging and inheritance are organized in Akan life. the way

Tjet — The Queen Mother (Bilabials):

In Egypt, the Tjet knot symbolized the feminine principle, protection, and life-force. In the Script, it governs the bilabials (M, B, P, F, W) - the sounds of the lips, the gate of nourishment, and speech.

Scepter — The King (Alveolars):

In Egypt, the scepter was the staff of rule and truth, the principle of authority and law. In the Script, it governs the alveolars (N, D, T, L, R, S) sounds placed with command and order.

Obelisk — The Priest (Velars):

The obelisk rose as a link between earth and sky, the human and the divine. In the Script, it governs the velars in succession G➜K➜H➜Y-sounds of depth, resonance, and vision from the throat.

Sankofa — The People (Vowels):

Sankofa is an Akan adinkra symbol, remembered in oral tradition and linked to the early adinkra work of leaders such as Nana Kwadwo. It means **"return and fetch it"** a call to remember what was lost, a symbol of purity and renewal. In the Script, it governs the vowels (A, E, I, O, U), the open breath that belongs to all people.

Together, these shelis echo the Abusua: queens, kings, priests, and people. The Abusua system was more than lineage; it was the architecture of order in Akan society. It bound people through blood, responsibility, and inheritance, weaving authority and belonging into a single covenant. Every person had a place, and every place carried both privilege and duty. By linking the shells to the Abusua, we don't alter the stroke itself; we reveal its resonance with a worldview where family is the root of balance and truth.

The Western way scatters vibration into fragments of borrowed letters. The Ananse Script gathers it back one line, one stroke, one web of order.

We will not go further into tones at this point. They will become much clearer once you've digested the rest of the writing system and seen how the pieces work together. Once you see how the pieces fit together, tones will be easier and more exciting to grasp. For now, placement and alteration are enough to carry you forward. And later, when we return to tones, you will recognize them not as a burden but as the final thread that completes the web.

If you wish to go deeper into the Abusua system and its richness, there are excellent references available. Below are two starting points you can read to understand more about the cultural, spiritual, and family depth of the Abusua system.

And with that, we turn to the first family of sounds, the Bilabials.

Inspired by google

Ananse Alphabet

Ananse Alphabet

A (Air Energy In Our Universe): A · E · I · O · U

M (Members Be Prepared For Winning): M · B · P · F · W

N (Nice Dogs Take Long Runs Swiftly): N · D · T · L · R · S

G (Greeting Kindly Honors You): G · K · H · Y

Remember: the mnemonics are your key.

Use them to understand the succession of sounds in each family.

With practice, the pattern will become second nature.

A · M · N · G

These are the four shells. All other sounds rest upon their foundation.

Bilabials

Question: Do you remember how bilabial sounds are formed?

Answer (in plain terms): They're made by pressing your two lips together. Every time you say M, B, P, F, W, you're closing and opening the lips to release sound.

In the Ananse Script, **M is the head**, which stands as pure potential.

Remember how we spoke about Russian dolls — one opening to reveal the next — or pressing piano keys in order? Bilabials follow the same logic. Once the **Ananse stroke** is placed — at the top, middle, or root — that single mark causes the potential in M to collapse into the other bilabial sounds, and the whole family is revealed.

One head, one stroke, and the whole family is revealed.

Reminder:

Even with their differences — F letting air escape with the bottom lip, and W rounding the lips outward — they still belong to the same house: sounds born from the lips.

Mnemonic:

"Members: Be Prepared For Winning."

Practice Box

Say each word out loud. Pay attention to each word — notice where your sound begins.

M: Man, Milk, Mother, Money
B: Boy, Book, Ball, Baby
P: Pen, Paper, Play, People
F: Food, Face, Fish, Friend
W: Water, Work, Window, World

Revealing the First Member of the Bilabial Family

When the bilabial shell (**M**) receives a stroke at the top, it awakens the sound **B** a voiced burst of the lips, the first member of the bilabial family.

This shows the power of the Ananse Stroke as the revealer: one shell, one stroke, and the hidden family begins to emerge.

B stands as the second sound of the bilabials, the first to be awakened when the stroke touches the head.

The **M shell stays M** on its own.

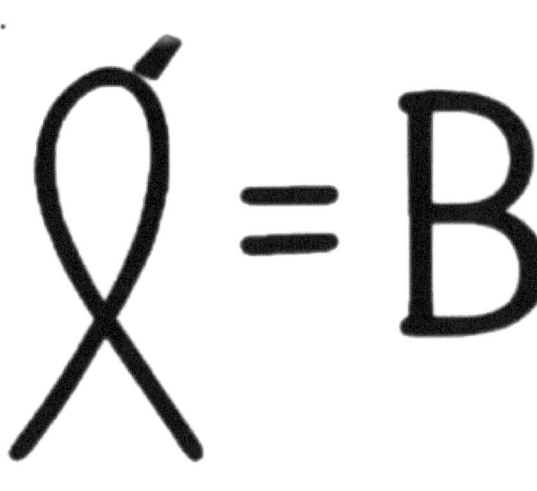

The sound **B** is the first to receive a stroke awakened when the stroke is placed at the top.

The Flow of the Stroke

As you can see, **the second member of the family has been revealed.** But this is only the beginning. The same process continues the Ananse stroke, placed in different locations on the shell, awakens each hidden member of the family.

When the stroke rests at the top, a new sound emerges. When it moves to the middle, another member is called forth. At the root, yet another comes alive, and with an extra stroke, even further members are revealed. One by one, from the same head, the family unfolds.

Think of it like a thread in a web: each placement connects differently, yet together they create a pattern of meaning. The head stands untouched, carrying the pure potential, while the stroke acts as the key that unlocks what is hidden within it.

Below, you will see this process in full. The shell of M, standing plain as the head, flows outward: first B, then P, then F, and finally W. What began as one becomes many. This is the rhythm of the Ananse Script: one stroke, many revelations.

Ancestral View of the Lip Sounds

We may understand the bilabial sounds as tied to the **maternal principle**. They carry inheritance, belonging, and spiritual continuity.

At the center of this principle stands the Queen Mother. She is not only the mother of a king but the spiritual anchor of the people. **The Queen Mother** carries the authority to name, to guide, and to speak truth to power. She is the voice of memory and continuity, guarding the line of descent, ensuring justice, and embodying compassion. Her presence is expected to nurture and protect, but also to hold rulers accountable to the people.

Thus, when we speak bilabials, we can let them remind us of this principle: that through the lips comes the rhythm of blood and milk, the pulse of the heart, and the nourishment of breath.

Through the bilabials, we connect sound with feeding, belonging, and continuity. In this way, the Queen Mother is reflected in the lips: **a source of life, care, and authority.**

From here, we move on to the Alveolar sound family, which is associated with kingship, the principle of rule, order, and leadership.

Q & A:

You've just worked with the first family born at the lips, the gateway of sound. They are simple, but never small; these are the sounds of closeness, of breath meeting breath. Now think ahead: what is the one language you would love to learn beyond your native tongue? Hold that in mind. Notice how often it begins with sounds at the lips— m, b, p. Training these here strengthens your foundation, making it easier to catch patterns and pronounce words more accurately when you approach that language. The real test, however, is just ahead. Turn the page, and let the questions show how much of this family you've already made your own.

Test Your Knowledge (Bilabials)

1. Which sound is the quiet head, standing alone until the stroke is placed?

2. When the stroke lands at the top, which sound bursts forth as the first revealed?

3. Think of the lips pressing together. Which family of sounds lives there?

4. Even though two of these sounds are different, escape with the teeth, the other rounds outward belong to the same family? one lets air, why do they still

5. How many members unfold from this head once the stroke is placed?

6. Can you still remember the rhythm of the mnemonic? Try reciting: "_____: Be Prepared For Winning."

Test Your Knowledge (Bilabials) – Answers

1. M — It is the head, standing alone until the stroke is placed.

2. B — It is the first sound revealed when the stroke lands at the top.

3. The Bilabials — sounds made with the lips pressing together.

4. Because both F and W still come from the lips - F lets air escape, W rounds outward, but both are born from the same house.

5. Five members unfold: M, B, P, F, and W.

6. "Members: Be Prepared For Winning."

Alveolars

Question: Do you remember what comes after the lips?

Answer (in plain terms): These sounds are made by your tongue tapping the ridge just behind your top teeth. Every time you say N, D, T, L, R, S, your tongue begins there.

Just like before, it's the same process. Think back to the Russian dolls or the piano keys. The Ananse Stroke works the same way, unfolding each sound in order. The only difference is that here the Alveolars have six family members, one more than the Bilabials.

In the Ananse Script, **N is the head** standing as pure potential.

Once the stroke is placed at the top, middle, or root, that potential collapses into the rest of the alveolar family, revealing them one by one.

One head, one stroke, and the whole family is revealed.

Mnemonic:

"Nice Dogs Take Long Runs Swiftly."

Reminder:

Even with their quirks, R curls or flicks the tongue, rolling the sound instead of pressing, and S doesn't tap at all, letting air hiss across the ridge like a secret whisper - they still belong to the same house: the tongue and the ridge just behind the teeth.

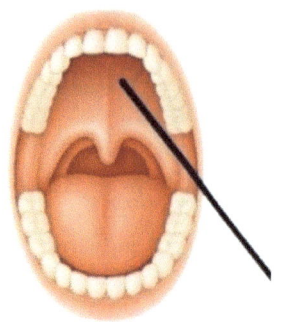

Say each word out loud. Pay attention to each word — notice where your tongue starts.

N: Name, Night, Number, Need

D: Door, Day, Drink, Dream

T: Time, Table, Talk, Town

L: Love, Life, Look, Light

R: Run, Rain, Road, River

S: Sun, Sit, Sing, School

Revealing the First Member of the Alveolar Family

When the alveolar shell (**N**) receives a stroke at the top, it awakens the sound **D**, a voiced tap of the ridge, the first member of the alveolar family.

This shows the power of the Ananse Stroke as the revealer: one shell, one stroke, and the hidden family begins to emerge.

N is the head, it stays N on its own, until the stroke is placed.

The sound D is the first to receive a stroke — awakened when the stroke is placed at the top.

Reminder: It's the same process across the board. The only difference is that the **Alveolars have six family members,** one more than the Bilabials.

N

N Stay N Without stroke

1 1́ = D

D is the first to receive the stroke, making it the second sound of the family.

The Flow of the Stroke (Alveolars)

Just as we saw with the bilabial sounds, the same process continues here. Even when the shell changes, the **Ananse Stroke** does not lose its power. It is the **Sound Organizer,** the one mark that keeps all sounds in check, placing them into their families.

When the stroke rests at the top of the alveolar shell (**N** as the head), it awakens **D**. When it moves to the middle, another member is called forth **T**. At the root, yet another is revealed **L**. With added curves and movement, the rest of the alveolar family emerges: **R** and **S**.

One by one, from the same head, the family unfolds.

Think of it as the staff of order: no matter where it strikes, it organizes what is hidden into a pattern of meaning. The head stands untouched, carrying pure potential, while the stroke reveals what is inside.

This is the rhythm of the Ananse Script: **one stroke, many revelations. The Sound Organizer, bringing voices into families.**

6 members, 1 shell

	1	=	N
Top	1́	=	D
Mid	1·	=	T
Root	1.	=	L
Root Xtra	1..	=	R
Root Xtra Xtra	1...	=	S

Alveolar family

Ancestral View of the Ridge Sounds (Alveolars)

You've heard about all the kings of the West; even today, people still hold kings and royalty in high respect. But what about kings in Africa? Have you heard of **Osei Tutu**, the Asante king of old?

He was remembered not only for his leadership but for the order he brought to his people. A king in Africa was not simply a figure of power; he was a protector, a judge, and a living symbol of the nation's strength. The people expected courage, fairness, and stability from him.

The alveolar sounds behind the teeth made by the tongue pressing the ridge can be seen as carrying this principle of kingship.

Just as the King strikes the staff on the ground to declare his authority, the tongue strikes the ridge to declare its sound.

So when we speak the alveolars N, D, T, L, R, S, we can let them remind us of the authority of the King. These sounds carry the spirit of rule and discipline, giving speech a sense of command and order.

Through the alveolars, we connect sound with leadership and kingship. In this way, the King is reflected in the ridge of the mouth: **a source of command, stability, and respect.**

Q & A

You've now reached the second family, the alveolars. These are the sounds made when the tongue taps the ridge just behind the teeth: *t, d, n, l, r, s*. They strike sharper than the bilabials, carrying clarity and precision. Here is a fact: across history, languages from Latin to Sanskrit to Twi have leaned heavily on these ridge-sounds. They are among the most stable sounds in human speech, carried from one language family to another without being lost. Training them here connects you to the same foundation spoken by millions across time. The questions ahead will show how well you've caught the rhythm of this family. Turn the page, and test how sharp your ear and memory have become.

Test Your Knowledge (Alveolars)

1. In the ancestral view of the Alveolars, which Ashanti king was remembered for his leadership and order?

2. Imagine the stroke landing at the bottom revealed from the ridge? which sound is

3. The Alveolars are the only family with one extra sound compared to the Bilabials. How many members do they hold in all?

4. Two members behave differently, one curls or flicks the tongue, the other hisses like a secret whisper. Can you name them?

5. When the tongue strikes just behind the teeth, what principle do the Alveolars remind us of?

6. Can you recall the rhythm of the mnemonic? Try reciting: "Nice _____ Take Long Runs _____."

Test Your Knowledge (Alveolars) - Answers

1. Osei Tutu- the Ashanti king remembered for his leadership and order.

2. L-it is the sound revealed when the stroke lands at the bottom.

3. Six members in total: N, D, T, L, R, and S.

4. R curls or flicks the tongue, while S lets air hiss like a secret whisper.

5. The principle of kingship - authority, rule, and order.

6. "Nice Dogs Take Long Runs Swiftly."

Who's ready for the Velar sound family?'

VELARS

Try this: Say the sound G out loud. Can't you tell where it's coming from?

Answer (in plain terms): Velar sounds are made at the back of the mouth, near the soft palate. Every time you say G, K, H, Y, the back of your tongue lifts toward the throat and releases the sound.

In the Ananse Script, **G is the head, which** stands as pure potential.

Imagine walking down a set of **four steps.** Each step brings you lower, unfolding what was hidden. The velar family works in the same way: once the Ananse stroke is **placed** at the top, middle, or root, the potential in G moves step by step into the other sounds, revealing the full family.

The velars are the **smallest family** of all, but even a small family holds great power.

Reminder:

Even with their differences — H releasing pure breath, and Y moving between vowel and consonant — they still belong to the same house:

sounds born from the throat.

Mnemonic:

"Greeting, Kindly Honors You."

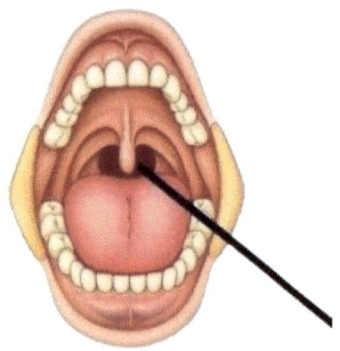

Practice Box

Say each word out loud. Pay attention to each word — notice where your sound begins.

G: Go, Give, Game, Girl

K: Keep, Kind, King, Kitchen

H: House, Hand, Help, Happy

Y: Yes, You, Young, Yellow

Revealing the First Member of the Velar Family

When the velar shell (**G**) receives a stroke at the top, it awakens the sound **K** a strike of the back of the tongue, the first member of the velar family.

This shows the power of the Ananse Stroke as the revealer: one shell, one stroke, and the hidden family begins to emerge.

G is the head — it stays G on its own, until the stroke is placed.

The sound **K** is the first to receive a stroke — awakened when the stroke is placed at the top.

Reminder: The Velars are the smallest family of sounds, but even a small family carries great power.

G stays G without the stroke.

K is the first to receive the stroke, making it the second member of the family.

The Flow of the Stroke (Velars)

As previously done twice before, we are seeing the pattern of the Ananse Stroke. It's law and order that never changes: one stroke, one head, many revelations.

When the stroke rests at the top, the first hidden member appears. When it moves to the middle, another sound is called forth. At the root, still another comes alive, and with extra movement, even the last members are revealed. One by one, from the same head, the family unfolds.

The Velars remind us that even the smallest family follows this law. The head remains untouched, carrying the pure potential, while the stroke brings the pattern of order, unlocking what is hidden within.

Below, you will see this process in full. The shell of G, standing plain as the head, flows outward: first K, then H, and finally Y. What began as one becomes many. This is the rhythm of the Ananse Script: law, order, and revelation.

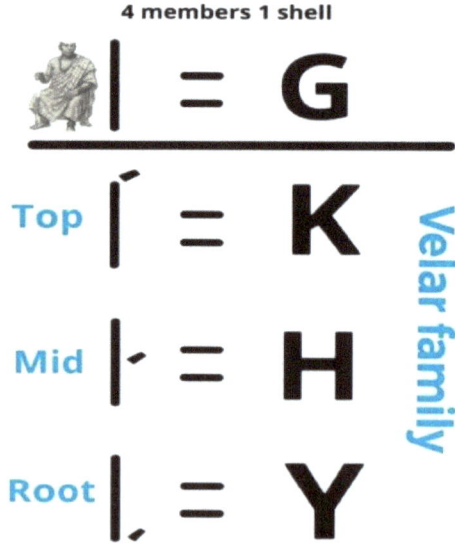

Ancestral View of the Throat Sounds (Velars)

You've heard about queens and kings. But what about those who stood between the people and the divine? Have you heard of **Okomfo Anokye**, the enigmatic West African priest remembered for his miracles, wisdom, and enduring spiritual impact?

He was more than a priest. He was a miracle-worker, a healer, a political genius, and a law-giver. The people saw him as the bridge between the ancestors and the living, the one who could summon sacred power to shape kingdoms and protect the nation. His role was to remind the people that there is more to life than what we see, and that words themselves carry spiritual force.

The velar sounds K, G, H, and Y made at the back of the mouth rise from deep within the throat. They carry this priestly weight: they are closer to the breath, closer to spirit.

Notice especially the sound **Y**. It stands on the border between consonant and vowel, able to belong to both families. This dual nature makes it the perfect sound to carry the principle of the priest: standing between two worlds, able to move in both directions, a voice of connection.

So when we speak the velars, we can let them remind us of the priestly role: to guide, to heal, to bridge heaven and earth.

Through the velars, we connect sound with wisdom, depth, and spirit. In this way, the Priest is reflected in the throat: a voice that calls the unseen into the seen.

Okomfo Anokye remains one of my favorite historical figures of West Africa, and if you've never heard his full story, I invite you to read of his amazing life and the wonders he performed.

Suggested Reading

Google inspired

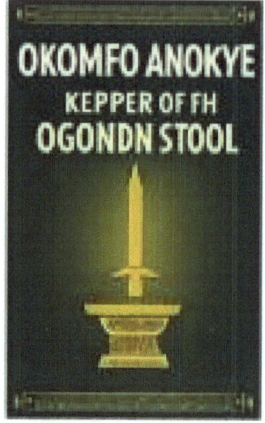

Check out the Actual book on Akomfo Anokye on Google

Q & A:

Y̲ou've arrived at the third family, the velars. These sounds rise from the back/high part of the tongue: k. g. y. They carry weight, shaping words with depth and resonance. Here is a fact: velars sit at the root of many languages. In Akan and Yoruba, they appear in words tied to spirit and creation. In Greek and Sanskrit, they mark some of the oldest root forms. Across cultures, words for kin, ground, and even God often begin here. Training these sounds links you to one of the deepest foundations in human speech. The answers ahead will show how well you've grounded this family in your own memory. Turn the page, and test how strong your foundation has become.

Test Your Knowledge (Velars)

1. When you said the sound **G** out loud earlier, where did you feel it begin?

2. There is one sound that never changes unless the stroke is placed. Which one was it?

3. Imagine those four steps again. Which sound takes the first step down from G?

4. Two members of this family are a little different; one is pure breath, the other stands between two worlds. Can you name them?

5. Even though this is the smallest family, what truth does it remind us of about power?

6. Can you still hear the rhythm of the mnemonic in your head? Try reciting: Kindly You."

Test Your Knowledge (Velars) – Answers

1. At the back of the mouth, near the soft palate.

2. G — it is the head, pure potential.

3. K — it is the first revealed when the stroke is placed, making it the second member of the family.

4. H (pure breath) and Y (moves between vowel and consonant).

5. That even a small family carries great power.

6. "Greeting Kindly Honors You."

Let's talk about Vowels, the open sound family.

VOWEL

VOWELS THE OPEN SOUNDS

We have journeyed through the consonant families:

- The lips gave us the Bilabials.
- The ridge behind the teeth gave us the Alveolars.
- The back of the throat gave us the Velars.

Each family was shaped by a point of contact: lips, tongue, teeth, or throat. But vowels are different.

Vowels are the open sounds. They are formed not by closing, tapping, or striking, but by leaving the mouth open and letting the breath flow free. They carry the pure tone of the voice, without obstruction.

Every language depends on vowels to keep its rhythm alive. They are the heartbeats of words, the voice that moves between consonants and makes speech possible. Without vowels, language collapses into whispers of broken edges.

In Akan, there are seven vowels. In English, there are five written vowels (A, E, I, O, U), but many more sounds when spoken. For clarity in this book, we focus on these five, the ones most readers already know.

If consonants are the bones of language, vowels are its **breath and spirit.**

Introduction & Mnemonic

"Air Energy In Our Universe."

Practice Box

Say each word out loud. Pay attention to each word — notice where your sound begins.

A: Apple, After, Ask, Able

E: Egg, End, Every, Enter

I: In, Inside, Into, Idea

O: Open, Over, Only, One

U: Up, Under, Us, Use

C

Stroke Unfolding (Head + Members)

Revealing the First Member of the Vowel Family

When the vowel shell (**A**) receives a stroke at the top, it awakens the sound **E,** an open sound of the breath, the first member of the vowel family.

This shows the power of the Ananse Stroke as the revealer: one shell, one stroke, and the hidden family begins to emerge.

A is the head —it stays A on its own, until the stroke is placed.

The sound **E** is the first to receive a stroke — awakened when the stroke is placed at the top.

Reminder: The vowels are the open sounds of language — pure breath and tone, carrying the rhythm of the people.

A stay A on it own

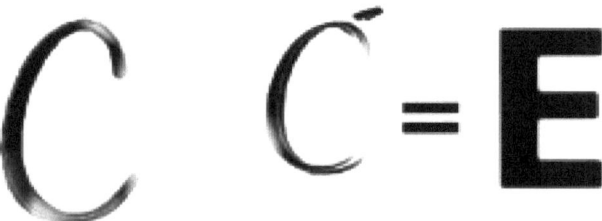

The sound **E** is the first to receive a stroke, making it the second member of the family.

Flow Of Stroke

The Flow of the Stroke (Vowels)

Oh no... not again! Hahaha. Yep, it's the same rule. Place the Ananse Stroke, and- boom-another sound shows up like it's been hiding there the whole time.

The head **A** is sitting there like, "Don't mind me, I'm just chilling." But once you place the stroke at the top, **E** pops out like, "Surprise, I'm here!" Move it to the middle, and I step in, like that friend who always shows up late but still gets the loudest hello. Drop the stroke to the root, and **O** comes rolling out-round, bold, impossible to ignore. And finally, twist it one more time, and **U** show up, waving like, "You didn't think I'd miss the party, right?"

See? Same law. Same order. Same magic trick. But hey, don't complain-it still works every time. The Ananse Stroke is nothing if not reliable.

Below, you will see this process in full. The shell of A, standing plain as the head, flows outward: first E, then I, then O, and finally U. What began as one becomes many. This is the rhythm of the Ananse Script, one stroke, many revelations... and a whole lot of personality.

	C	= **A**
Top	C	= E
Mid	C·	= I
Root	C.	= O
Root Xtra	C..	= U

VOWEL FAMILY

Ancestral/Culture View (Queen, King, Priest, People)

Ancestral View of the Open Sounds (Vowels)

We have just spoken of **Okomfo Anokye** and the priestly powers of old. But before we move into the vowels, the sounds of the people, we must pause and look with clear eyes at where we stand today.

Ninety-nine percent of what is called African spirituality in our time is a far cry from its purest form. Too often it follows the path laid down by Christianity: money for prayers, vibration without transformation. The deeper essence of the balance of life, the connection to Ancestors, the order of spirit has been broken.

When the Europeans enslaved us, they did not capture a people at their highest. We were already **fallen people**. West Africa's struggles for power, its rivalries and wars, cannot be mistaken for the fullness of Africa's way of life. If we stop there, we see only fragments.

To understand the people, we must delve deeper and look further back. We must return to **East Africa, to Kemet, to the giants of Sudan, to the far edges of South Africa, the cradle of civilization itself, and more.**

Think of men like **Dr. Yosef Ben-Jochannan (Dr. Ben)** and **Professor John Henrik Clarke** — historians who spoke without compromise. Imagine being blinded by age, but never silenced from speaking truth. These were men who carried light into a world of distortion, reminding us of who we were before the fall.

And we cannot forget the **Ashanti Kingdom**, which rose with its people, carried forward by their discipline, unity, and resilience. The Ashanti were not defined by kings alone, but by the strength of their people, their devotion to order, and their connection to their Ancestors.

Practice & Q&A (With Spider Encouragement)

Q & A:

You've reached the last family of the vowels. Unlike the consonants, they are not shaped by lips, teeth, or ridge, but by the open breath itself: *a, e, i, o, u*. They stand as pure sound, the voice uncovered. Here is a fact: every known language relies on vowels. Some have as few as three, others more than a dozen, but none are without them. They are the lifeblood of words, carrying tone, emotion, and rhythm across cultures. Training them here strengthens your ability to hear and reproduce the subtle differences that make languages distinct. The questions ahead will show how well you can hold the shape of these open sounds. Turn the page, and test how fully you've grasped the head of the language.

Test Your Knowledge (Vowels)

1. Which vowel sits as the quiet head, staying still until the stroke is placed?

2. When the stroke rests at the top, which sound jumps out first, making it the second member of the family?

3. Move the stroke to the middle, which sound is revealed there?

4. Drop the stroke to the root, which rounds the sound rolls into place?

5. And finally, with one more turn, which vowel waves and says, "You didn't think I'd miss the party, right?" what makes them

6. Why are the vowels called the open sounds different from the consonant families like Bilabials, Alveolars, and Velars?

7. Can you recall the mnemonic for the vowels? Try reciting: "Air ___ in our ___."

Test Your Knowledge

Integration

Our Test Your Knowledge (Vowels) - Answers

1. A — It is the head, staying still until the stroke is placed.

2. E — it is the first to receive a stroke, making it the second member of the family.

3. I — revealed when the stroke is placed in the middle.

4. O — the round sound that rolls in at the root.

5. U — the last to appear, waving as the final member of the vowel family.

6. Vowels are called the open sounds because they are made without blocking or striking, just pure breath and voice flowing freely, unlike consonant families that rely on contact points.

7. "Air Energy In Our Universe."

From here, we move on to how it all ties together.

A REMINDER

The symbols repeat. There are only four shells to look at.

Your eyes have been trained to expect variety, the 26 letters of the alphabet, and variety creates the illusion that memorization is easy. Here, the strength is different: the Ananse stroke moves in only three placements.

At first, this feels unnatural. But with practice, the eye adjusts, and what looks repetitive now will soon feel natural.

This is only a hurdle, and it will be jumped with ease.

Think of it like music. At first, the notes look like marks on a page. But once you learn the scale, every song makes sense. The Ananse Writing System works the same way. Once you learn the families and where the stroke belongs, your mind and eyes flow together. You no longer ask, "What is this character?" You already know.

This is the gift of the Ananse Writing System: **clarity through order, simplicity through law, and freedom through understanding.**

Word of Encouragement

If you find yourself struggling here, pause and breathe. You are not failing, you are entering something new.

Remember, this system is not built to look familiar. It is built to **reveal law beneath appearance.** To those raised in the alphabet of 26 scattered letters, writing with four shells may

feel awkward, even unnecessary. The shells may seem redundant. The stroke may feel like an extra mark. The system may feel foreign.

But that discomfort is the proof that you are learning.

Every tradition of initiation begins with resistance: the mind wants to return to the old ways. But if you stay with it, the old breaks open and the new pattern appears. With practice, you will begin to see not 26 fragments, but **four roots unfolding into families.** Not clutter, but clarity.

You are training your mind to move differently: not to memorize letters, but to **think in categories, patterns, and laws of succession.** This is the very gift of the Ananse Script.

So do not be discouraged if your hand hesitates or your mind feels lost. You are walking a path once hidden. What feels foreign today will become natural tomorrow. With each stroke, you are not just writing, you are building a new way of seeing.

How It All Ties Together-Lip, Ridge, Throat, Breath as Web

From the vowels, the breath of speech,

to the lips, where sound takes form.

From the ridge behind the teeth, where order is struck,

to the deep of the tongue, where spirit is carried.

Together, they are not fragments,

but a web one line, many voices.

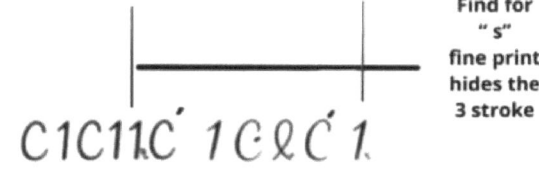

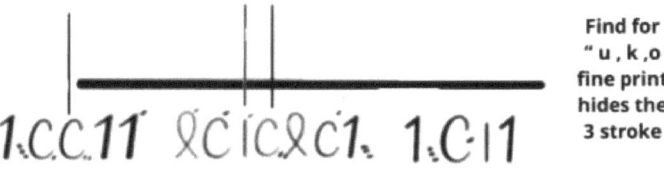

Notice how **Ananse** simplifies spelling.

Life ➜ l ifes (not lives)

Becomes ➜ bekoms (silent 'e' dropped)

English is filled with irregularities, shaped by Old English mixing with French and other languages. These irregular spellings were compromises, not pure sound. **Ananse avoids this.**

The plural and other forms stay close to the **base sound**, keeping language simple and logical.

Test Your Knowledge - Recap

1. Why is the Ananse Stroke important in the writing system?

2. What are the two main purposes of the Ananse Stroke?

3. How does the Stroke act as a "Sound Organizer" for the different families?

4. Which sounds stand as the heads of the Bilabials, Alveolars, Velars, and Vowels?

5. Why do we say that vowels are the "open sounds" of language?

6. Beyond sound, what cultural or ancestral principles do the three consonant families (Bilabials, Alveolars, Velars) remind us of?

Test Your Knowledge Recap (Answers)

1. Because it brings law and order to the system, revealing hidden members of each family and keeping sounds organized.

2. (a) To reveal the members of a sound family. (b) To show tone high, mid, or low.

3. By being placed at the top, middle, or root, the stroke keeps the families in order and ensures every sound has its place.

4. Bilabials: M | Alveolars: N I Velars: G I Vowels: A

5. Because they are formed without closing or striking, just open breath and voice flow freely.

6. Bilabials = Queen Mother (care, nurture, continuity). Alveolars = Kingship (order, rule, authority). Velars = Priesthood (wisdom, spirit, guidance).

Surprise: Try These Words

Using the Ananse Script

A: ____ ____ ____ ____

        (Air Energy In Our Universe)

M: ____ ____ ____ ____

        (Members Be Prepared For Winning)

N: ____ ____ ____ ____

        (Nice Dogs Take Long Runs Swiftly)

G: ____ ____ ____ ____

        (Greeting Kindly Honors You)

"Use mnemonics"

1. I_____

2. We_____

3. you_____

4. he_____

5. play_____

6. come_____

7. look_____

8. sing_____

Writing practice

9. walk_____

10. she_____

11. it_____

12. go_____

13. run_____

14. jump_____

15. eat_____

16. drink_____

17. read_____

18. write_____

19. talk_____

Enjoy with friends

Writing practice

20. laugh_____

21. sleep_____

22. love_____

23. help_____

24. give_____

25. take_____

26. sit_____

27. stand_____

28. open_____

29. close_____

30. family_____

31. people_____

32. school_____

33. mother_____

34. father_____

35. sister_____

36. brother_____

37. garden_____

38. market_____

39. village_____

40. teacher_____

41. student_____

42. animal_____

43. country_____

44. culture_____

45. language_____

46. freedom_____

47. history_____

48. tomorrow_____

49. together_____

Sound Weaver-Title and Quantum Bridge

Congratulations, Sound Weaver

You have walked through the gates of sound — the lips, the ridge, and the throat. You have seen how the Ananse Stroke brings law and order, unfolding families one by one. You have practiced, reflected, and tested yourself.

Now pause and give yourself credit. Many begin this journey, but few take it seriously enough to reach this point. By completing these pages, you have stepped into the work of a **Sound Weaver** — who can see patterns, understand families, and hear the hidden rhythm in language.

This is more than language. What you've just done is **pattern recognition** — the ability to see order inside what looks like chaos. That same skill is the foundation of the world's most advanced science: **quantum computing**.

Just as the Ananse Stroke organizes sounds into families, quantum rules organize particles into possibilities. Both ask us to think beyond the surface, to see the hidden structure that gives life its rhythm.

So wear your new title with honor: **Sound Weaver of the Ananse Script.**

And now, let's step forward together from sound to systems, from lips and tongue to quantum bits.

Next: **Quantum Computing: The Pattern Behind the Pattern.**

BEYOND WRITING: QUANTUM & PRIVACY

Ananse & Quantum Computing- Shells as Quantum States

We've been talking about shells, strokes, and families — a writing systems born from sound and order. Now, you might wonder, "What could this possibly have to do with computers, let alone quantum physics?" Fair question.

Here's the surprise: the same logic that makes Ananse Script work on the page also echoes how scientists describe reality itself. When physicists talk about quantum states and quantum gates, they sound a lot like what we've just seen with shells and strokes. It's almost as if the ancestors built a quantum model long before laptops and labs.

The four shells of Ananse work like quantum states: each one holds potential, waiting to be released. The three stroke placements act like quantum gates: they don't invent something new, but reveal what was already there. Press the shell alone and you get its base sound. Add a stroke, and the potential resolves into clarity like a quantum system choosing one outcome.

Bilabial shell (M) → base state.

Top stroke (B) → revealed state.

Middle stroke (P) → alternate resolution.

Breath shell (vowels) the current of air that carries sound forward.

These sounds already lived inside the shell. The stroke simply decides which version of reality comes forward.

This is why Ananse belongs to the future. Quantum computing should not waste computing power on messy alphabets or arbitrary shapes. It needs a system that is minimal, logical, and collapses cleanly. With only four shells and three strokes, Ananse provides exactly that.

In other words:

Ananse is a quantum alphabet. The shells hold all sounds in superposition; the strokes resolve them into the exact expressions we need.

For humans, this makes writing natural. For AI and quantum machines, it makes language efficient and unambiguous. **Ananse collapses thought into clear signals without waste.** It is not just another script - it is the bridge between speech and the quantum age.

Quantum computing is already part of today's technology, precise and powerful. That is the serious side of the future. But not all technology carries that weight. Some of it is meant to be light, playful, and even fun.

Think about the gadgets shaping everyday life: smart glasses that blend digital with reality, AI that responds before you finish asking, and games that teach while entertaining. The value of Ananse here is not about going faster, but about using less computing power, working with greater efficiency, and creating a bridge where humans are not overwhelmed.

So let's turn to some of that cool tech, the Meta glasses, and a few more tools that show how Ananse can step right into the world we're building.

Ananse Keyword - Interface Of The Future

Ananse Keyboard, Meta Glasses / AI And Games

Choosing a Reserved Life and Gadgets

I have chosen a more reserved way of life for myself, yet I must admit: certain gadgets remain part of my world.

They draw me in not for their glitter, but for the ground-breaking discoveries they represent.

And when I think of computers, I do not think of them as only machines. I attach them to the spiritual domain. Circuits are like veins of energy.

Binary Code and Ifá Divination

Binary code is nothing new it is the same casting of opposites, the same pairing of possibility, that the Babalawo has practiced for centuries through Ifá divination.

Before man ever imagined a computer, Ifá was already showing how signs combine, how destiny is written, how knowledge hides in code.

The Abusua System as a Code

Alongside Ifá, the Abusua system of clans is itself a code a logic of belonging and inheritance, a structure that encodes order into society just as programming encodes order into machines.

Global Traditions of Encoding Knowledge

These patterns are not African alone:

- India: The ancient Vedas encoded vast spiritual and mathematical knowledge into hymns and meter algorithms sung in rhythm, a living archive of memory and logic.
- China: Scholars shaped the I Ching, a binary system of broken and unbroken lines that mapped possibility, a mirror of both destiny and computation.
- Mayan World: Priests carved calendars and codes of time into stone, encoding cycles of the cosmos with precision so deep that they still astonish us today.
- Australia: The Aboriginal peoples carried knowledge through Songlines — maps of land, law, and ancestry sung across the continent, a living database that turned geography itself into code.

From Spirit to Machines

Only after spirit and society gave these patterns did men put them into metal and gears.

The Pioneers of Modern Computation

Then came the pioneers:

- Charles Babbage (1837): Outlined the Analytical Engine, the first description of a programmable machine.
- Ada Lovelace (1843): Wrote the first algorithm, proving that numbers could carry meaning beyond calculation.
- Herman Hollerith (1890): Built the punch card system that processed the U.S. Census, translating information into machine-readable form.
- Alan Turing (1936): Described the Turing Machine, laying the theoretical foundation.

Continuations of Ancestral Codes

for modern computing and showing how thought itself could be mirrored in steps of logic. Each of these breakthroughs was a thread, but never the first thread. They were continuations, resting on the web the Ancestors already spun: the Ifá chain, the Abusua code of kinship, the hymns of the Vedas, the hexagrams of the I Ching, the Mayan calendar, the Aboriginal Songlines, the rhythms of nature, and even the very cell dividing to carry its instructions.

Join me in a pause of gratitude: for the wisdom of Ifá, for the Abusua that encodes family and order, for the Vedic seers of India, the sages of China, the Mayan timekeepers, the Aboriginal custodians of Songlines, for the pioneers who carried it forward, and for the unseen worlds above and beneath us that still whisper the same truth. All of these are foundations for the path we walk today.

And as you pause, feel the thread of your own life within this same web. You, too, are part of the code; your choices, your gifts, your roles all carry memory forward.

Now, with that awareness alive in us, we step forward into the living weave of Ananse. Here, the story does not end with memory or myth. It reappears in the Keyboard that encodes sound, the Meta glasses that expand vision, and the games that guide children into discovery. Each is a strand of the same web — spun long ago, still growing, and you are already within it.

On to the Keyboard, shall we?!

Meta & AI

Continuation of Ananse Keyboard, Meta Glasses, AI, and Kids' Games

The English Keyboard vs. Ananse Script

Think of the English keyboard you type on every day: 26 scattered letters, extra keys, symbols, and redundancies. Each one must be memorized separately, pressed separately. The mind carries dead weight. Now imagine a different approach: instead of 26+ keys, you need only four shells - A, M, N, G and a handful of strokes. With this, the Ananse Script unlocks every sound. One base + one stroke = one revelation. Where English gives you clutter, Ananse gives you compression. Where English gives you repetition, Ananse gives you rhythm. Where English gives you 26 scattered signs, Ananse gives you four shells, infinite families.

Example of Families

Your example: Start with M. Add a top stroke B. Add a middle stroke = P. Add a root stroke = F. Add an extra root stroke = W. In four moves, you have a family. Instead of memorizing 26+ random keys, your mind learns only four homes and their rules.

The result is a keyboard that is lighter, faster, and more abstractly designed, not just for humans, but ready for AI.

Meta Glasses: The Human Interface

Now lift your eyes. What if the keyboard were no longer under your fingers, but floating before your vision? With Meta's Ray-Ban Display and Neural Band control, the Ananse Script becomes a human interface: Left hand shells (A, M, N, G): thumb taps summon the heads. - Right-hand strokes: top, middle, root, or extra taps complete the family. Example: You tap N with your left hand. Add a middle stroke with your right thumb, and the letter T appears in the lens. Tap again, and another member of the family reveals itself. The effect: Text input becomes invisible. Writing is faster, smoother, and balanced across both hands. Words appear as thought itself, even without opening your eyes.

AI: A Tool Worth Considering

If AI today is drowning in too many signs, Ananse shows how less can be. more. Instead of memorizing thousands of disconnected letters and redundancies, Ananse compresses. Its generative rules mirror supercomputing and quantum logic: fewer signs, more meaning. This makes it a framework worth considering for an AI pattern-based, efficient, and memory-light. By mirroring ancient codes (Ifá, Abusua, Vedas, I Ching, Mayan glyphs, Songlines), the Ananse Script shows how machines too can learn with less burden, more rhythm.

The Challenge: Children and the Shells

Now imagine a child with the Ananse Script. Example: The child presses A. - They add a stroke, and suddenly a vowel family unfolds. They ask, "What happens if I add another? What if I do it faster? Can I do it with my eyes closed?" Each tap becomes a question. Each question becomes a discovery. Instead of rote memorization, children learn through exploration and play, the natural way the human brain grows.

The Promise

Whether for AI, wearable interfaces, or childhood growth, the Ananse Script is not just a writing system. It is a bridge lighter, faster, patterned, carrying wisdom from Ancestors into the tools of tomorrow.

Private System - Personal Cipher, Shared Bridge

The Ananse Script as a Private System

If you recall, I mentioned earlier that an app is in the works for this writing system. This is more than just a digital tool — it's the way Ananse comes alive in our time. And one of its most powerful features is privacy woven into the act of writing itself. The app will allow every user to choose their own four shells — the foundation characters that anchor the system. Once the rules of Ananse are understood, the actual symbols become flexible. You can discard your set of shells and select four new ones at any time. The stroke system remains unchanged, meaning you will always be able to read and write fluently, no matter which characters are chosen. This creates a layer of privacy that is both subtle and powerful. If someone were to glance at your phone, your tablet, or your computer screen, they would see writing that appears foreign — symbols with no obvious connection to the words you know. To anyone outside your circle, your script is unreadable. To you and those you've shared your shells with, it is perfectly clear. Privacy here is not only technical; it is relational. A husband and wife might choose their own four shells, making their conversations instantly private. A company or a creative team might establish their own internal script, giving them a language of belonging and confidentiality. Two friends across the world might share their shells and know that they are communicating in a private space, invisible to outsiders. In time, it is not the letters themselves that matter, but the way the strokes fall. The shells are simply the doorway. What keeps your script private is that no one else knows your chosen four — unless you invite them in. This makes Ananse not just a tool for writing, but a world of personal lettering, alongside a shared standard system that the masses can use for open communication. But privacy can deepen further. Over time, the rules of the strokes themselves can also be changed. In one system, the top stroke may represent one sound; in another, it may represent a different one. The families remain, but their order bends to your design. To the outsider, the writing looks familiar, yet its meaning has shifted beneath the surface. This becomes an extra layer of privacy — not only personal shells, but personal grammar. Even if someone learned your four shells, they would still need to know your unique rule-set to read your script. Privacy here is not static but evolving, adaptable, and alive. In such a world, every individual could carry two scripts at once: the shared public standard for open communication, and their private Ananse for intimacy, trust, and identity. It is writing as a universal bridge, and writing as a personal cipher — both at the same time. And perhaps that is the quiet reminder Ananse leaves us with: in an age where everything is exposed, recorded, and shared, the most valuable possession is not what we publish, but what we protect. Privacy is not secrecy — it is freedom. It is the ability to decide what belongs to the world and what belongs only to you. The Ananse Script carries this truth into writing. To hold your own shells, to choose your own rules, to decide who may enter your circle — this is not just convenience. It is power. It is dignity. It is the whisper that not all doors should stand open, and that some words are strongest when they are yours alone.

COMPARATIVE LINGUISTICS & CRITIQUE

Minimalism, Hangeul, and Chomsky on the Ananse Script

Noam Chomsky once asked a deceptively simple question: What is the smallest system of rules that can generate the infinite variety of human language? This question split the linguistic community. On one side, behaviorists and empiricists argued that language is learned from the environment - shaped by imitation, repetition, and culture. On the other hand, Chomsky proposed that language is an innate biological faculty, built on a Universal Grammar that all humans share. His Minimalist Program took this further, suggesting that beneath the surface complexity of language lies a small set of powerful, elegant rules. The debate has never been fully settled. Both perspectives have weight.

Language is clearly shaped by social environment and cultural context, yet it also seems to unfold in ways too rapid and universal to be explained by exposure alone. I find myself in the middle of this conversation. I understand the relevance of both positions. Yet I resonate with Chomsky's minimalism: the belief that the greatest variety of expression can emerge from the smallest and simplest system.

This is where the Ananse Script enters. It echoes Chomsky's vision not through grammar, but through writing. Instead of 26 scattered letters or dozens of memorized shapes, it begins with four shells and a single stroke placed in three positions. From this compressed structure, entire families of sounds unfold. Other traditions have sought this kind of economy.

Hangeul, the Korean script created in the 15th century under King Sejong, was designed with good intentions: to give common people a way to read and write in a society where Chinese characters were too complex and restricted to elites. Hangeul is admired for its science. Its consonants are modeled after the shape of the lips, tongue, and throat, and its vowels reflect the sky, earth, and human. It is a democratic script - simple in concept, socially revolutionary, and deeply tied to the body.

And yet, even Hangeul is not free of flaws. It requires more than forty distinct shapes, which, though logical in design, still create redundancy. Some characters are considered faulty, overlapping in sound or function, and the learner must still memorize far more than is necessary. For all its brilliance, Hangeul carries weight.

Here is where the Ananse Script shows its difference. By compressing to four shells and a stroke, it reduces the burden by as much as 80% compared to Hangeul or English. It is not completely linguistically precise, it does not attempt to represent every manner of articulation, but that is its strength. It compresses, and it trusts context, tone, and accent to do what overcomplicated systems attempt to force through extra symbols.

Even in English, many spellings do not match pronunciation. We already rely on context to read correctly. Ananse makes this principle explicit. Where Hangeul sought to simplify access for commoners, Ananse seeks to compress knowledge for everyone, commoner, scholar, child, or even AI. It removes the unnecessary, honors the natural families of sound, and leaves only what is needed for clarity.

Where Chomsky gave us Merge, the simplest operation joining two units into one, Ananse gives us the stroke, a single motion that unlocks sound families. Both reveal the same principle: clarity is not weakness but strength. From the fewest rules, the widest possibilities arise.

The Ananse Script does not force us to choose between biology and environment. It is grounded in the body, lips, tongue, throat, breath - like Hangeul. But it also embodies the minimalist code Chomsky described: a handful of rules generating infinite variety. And so we return to the seed. Chomsky searched for the smallest grammar. Hangul gave us a scientific map of the body. Ananse gives us the smallest script: four shells, one stroke, three positions. Not burden, but lift. Not clutter, but clarity.

The smallest seed grows the largest tree. If the Ananse Script shows how clarity in symbols can lift the burden of writing, then the next step is to see how clarity can also transform spelling. Just as sounds can be compressed into families, words themselves can be carried along dual paths, a system that balances minimal rules with the fullness of meaning.

Dual Path- Traditional Vs Ananse Simplicity

Dual Path Spelling Next

The Burden of English Spelling

If the Ananse Script shows how clarity in symbols can lift the burden of writing, then spelling, too, must be brought into the same light. For centuries, English has carried the weight of irregular forms, silent letters that no longer serve sound, overlapping symbols that repeat one another, and spellings that drift far from the way people actually speak.

Tradition and Its Weight

What began as a habit has hardened into a tradition. Tradition has its place. The old spellings connect us to our history, to the words of poets and scriptures, to libraries and law. But this weight also slows the learner, confuses the child, and even burdens the machine. English has often preserved form at the cost of clarity. Even the scholars who guard the language have known its troubles.

Attempts at Reform

Over the centuries, many have tried to smooth the rough edges, cutting silent letters, proposing phonetic alphabets, or reshaping rules. But these efforts were piecemeal. They "dibble and dabble," never bold enough to complete the work. Some reforms were too fractured, others too rigid, and all met with resistance from readers who were already bound to the spellings they knew.

The Result of Tradition

The result is a spelling system that is clever in history

The Ananse Script's Approach

The Ananse Script moves differently. It refuses to waste. One sound, one spelling. No ghosts, no clutter. Each mark must serve the living voice. Each stroke must carry sound directly, not trail centuries of duplication.

Space for Two Paths

And yet Ananse does not demand that history be erased. It leaves room for two paths:

One that keeps traditional spelling alive for those who wish to honor continuity.

Another that simplifies for children, learners, and even machines, where speed and clarity matter most.

Principle of Dual Path Spelling

Both paths tell the same word. Both lead to the same meaning. But one carries less burden and arrives with greater ease. This is the principle of Dual Path Spelling to hold tradition in one hand and clarity in the other, letting every reader, every teacher, and every system choose their path while knowing that both roads meet at the same destination.

Closing

Turn the page to see the chart that brings these paths side by side.

This work honors every language and its history. It is not an attack on English or tradition; it is a step toward **clarity**, toward writing that matches how people speak and how children learn.

Why English Feels Heavy

English spelling is rich in history, but also rich in **irregularity.** The same sound appears under many spellings, and the same letter holds many sounds. To cover these gaps. English creates rules on top of exceptions, which confuses children, slows learners, and even burdens machines.

Examples of Unnecessary Symbols (kept for tradition, not sound):

C ➜ use **K** (cat kaf) or **S** (city ➜ sity).

Q ➜ really **KW** (quick ➜ Awk).

X ➜ **KS** (fox foks) or **Z** (xylophone ➜ zylophone).

GH ➜ silent or becomes **F** (though ➜ tho, laugh laf).

PH ➜ just **F** (phone ➜ fon).

KN ➜ silent **K** (knight ➜ nite)

WH ➜ simply **W** (what ➜ wat).

Silent E ➜ dropped when it adds no sound (name ➜ naim).

Ananse's Answer

The Ananse Script removes this dead weight. One sound, one spelling. No silent letters. No wasted symbols. Instead of making up rules to fit irregularity, Ananse **removes** the irregularity so rules are barely needed.

Dual Path Spelling

Ananse does not demand we abandon tradition. There are two paths to writing the same word: **Traditional Spelling** (historic forms) and **Ananse Spelling** (soundtruth, simple, direct). Both reach the meaning, but the simpler path builds clarity faster for children and machines.

Word	Traditional Spelling	Anansi Spelling	Notes
Thought	thought	thot	Silent "gh" removed; sound stays the same.
Through	through	thru	Four extra letters cut away; true sound remains.
Though	though	tho	One clean vowel replaces confusing "ough."
Phone	phone	fon	"Ph" changes to the real sound /f/.
Knight	knight	nite	Silent "k" and "gh" vanish, leaving the sound only.
Laugh	laugh	laf	"gh" removed; sound written directly.

Why This Matters

Differentiation In Ananse- Homograpgh, Homophones, Context

Differentiation In Ananse

But spelling is only half the challenge. Languages also throw curveballs with words that look the same but mean different things. and words that sound the same but have different spellings. English solves this with clutter. Ananse solves it with clarity. To see how, we must step into the world of homographs, homophones, and the context areas that give them meaning.

Ananse takes what humans already do in speech and makes it the law of writing.

And don't worry, I'll break that down for you after defining these linguistic terms.

> **Disclaimer: Read Before Entering This Section**
> - **Homographs** → Same spelling, different meanings. *One word, two lives.*
> - **Homophones** → Same sound, different spellings. *Different clothes, same voice.*
> - **Context Areas** → The natural guides — sentence, tone, and subject. *The gentle hints your mind already knows how to use.*

The English Problem

- **Homographs** ➜ Words like lead, tear, row force learners to memorize unpredictable pronunciations.
- **Homophones** ➜ Words like right, write, rite make learners juggle multiple spellings for one sound.

This creates clutter, wasted memory, and endless exceptions.

The Ananse Solution

Homographs (Double Agents)

Examples: lead (guide/metal), tear (drop/rip), row (line/argument).

Ananse Way: Collapse into one spelling.

- Primary guide = context areas (sentence, tone, subject).
- Secondary guides the stroke itself, curved up, flat, or down, when extra clarity is needed.

Homophones (Copycats)

Examples: right/write/rite, pair/pear, sea / see. Ananse Way: Collapse into one spelling (rit, per, si).

- Primary guide = context areas.
- Secondary guide stroke variation, if needed, to mark subtle differences without clutter.

Ananse does not add spellings- it trusts the brain and, if necessary, lets the stroke step in.

Context Areas (The Gentle Guides)

When spelling is simplified, meaning doesn't vanish; it shifts into context, where it belongs.

Three main areas of context:

- Sentence ➜ The words around it: "She will rit her name" vs. "That is the rit answer."
- Tone ➜ The rise or fall of voice adds flavor.
- Subject ➜ The topic sharpens meaning: in school, rit write; in morality, rit right.

In Ananse, context replaces clutter, while the stroke is always available as backup.

Why Ananse is Greater

English multiplies spellings, exceptions, and confusion.

Ananse multiplies clarity.

- English: Different spellings, same sound → heavy memorization.
- Ananse: One spelling, one sound and tone → with stroke variation for precision. meaning clear through context

Ananse doesn't reinvent the human mind. It trusts it. It takes what people already do in speech every day and makes it the law of writing.

Stroke Differentiation in Action

(Use this space to practice how the stroke clarifies meaning)

- Curve Up → **Right**   Rit'
- Flat → **Rite**   Rit-
- Curve Down → **Write**   Rit

What we've just seen is how Ananse clears away English clutter, one spelling, one sound, with context and the stroke handling meaning. But English isn't the only language that carries baggage. French, for all its beauty, has long lived with silent letters and ornamental spellings. Yet even French proves something important: fewer letters can still carry full meaning. That's where we turn next to the French Connection.

French Connection- Elegance, Excess, And Hidden Hypocrisy

French Connection Excess Elegance

Introduction: French as the Courtier

French is a language of elegance. It dresses words in silent letters and accents, preserving history in every line.

Beautiful, yes, but heavy. To learn French is to memorize relics.

And yet, beneath these ornaments lies a truth: French already

hints at the law of Ananse. With just a small stroke, an accent can shift meaning: é versus è. With liaison, context rules over spelling: les amis becomes lez-ami. Even its silent letters prove that sense can survive without excess.

These are fragments of the same principle Ananse declares openly: clarity through minimal marks, meaning guided by context. In this way, French and Ananse are relatable; both show how a single stroke or shift can carry a world of meaning.

But that does not mean French is free from burden. Elegance has its price. And that brings us to a question.

Do You See a Problem?

Do you see a problem within the French system of speaking and writing? At first glance, it appears refined, admired across the world. But when we look closer, we find issues that weigh especially on the young, who must carry not just sound, but centuries of ornament preserved as relics.

- **Silent Letters:** words like fils or chevaux carry letters never spoken.
- **Ornamental Endings:** grand keeps its d, though it adds nothing to sound.
- **Over-Agreement:** verbs bend again and again for gender and number, even when speech is already clear.

What learners struggle to memorize is not sound or meaning, but the weight of tradition. These marks remain not because they are needed for clarity, but because they are revered. France insists on carrying its past forward, showing how deeply it esteems its own history, and that is exactly what we, too, must reclaim, for our history was targeted, broken, and denied the same right of continuity.

The French Lesson

Accents, Strokes → one mark shifts the sound (é, é, é).

Liaison = Context → les amis → les amis. Spelling obeys flow.

Silent Letters =Proof→ meaning survives without them.

Here, French hints at what Ananse makes law: clarity does not need clutter. A minimal mark can guide sound, context can complete meaning, and language can thrive without excess.

Ananse's Answer

Where French hesitates, Ananse fulfills:

- One Stroke = Many Accents Unified.
- Context First, Mark Second.
- Every Symbol Speaks — no silent shells..

The Hidden Hypocrisy

Now pause here and look closer. Even the smallest marks of French and English are carried forward as treasures, not for sound, but for memory.

And they are not alone. The Chinese preserve their characters, the Japanese keep Kanji and Katakana, and the Indians protect Sanskrit. Across Asia, systems are preserved as sacred. Ethiopia, too, maintains its own script, rare on the African continent.

But Africa at large was told to abandon its relics. Our systems of writing and memory were outlawed, our connections to our true selves cut, and we were forced into Western scripts and operating systems. What others were praised for protecting, we were punished for keeping. That is the hypocrisy.

Now pause again and look wider. Let's turn to another relic they choose to acknowledge: slavery.

They will admit it happened, yes, you were enslaved. But notice the frame. The admission is quickly followed by a new story: slavery is over, you have been uplifted, and equality is here. The very act of confessing becomes a way of hiding.

What they do not say is that slavery has not disappeared; it has shifted. The chains no longer bind the body, but the psyche. The ship no longer sails the seas, but drifts in policies, schools, and systems. What was once iron is now narrative.

Yet what they cannot erase is frequency. Rhythm cannot be outlawed. Memory cannot be destroyed. The ancestral current flows beneath every attempt at control.

This is why the West tries to cast us as the global delinquent, the people forever broken, forever in need of guidance, while pretending no role in the destruction. But it is only a projection. The story they write about us is not the truth of who we are.

From the West to Our Truth

This is not just about letters. It is about systems' entire architectures of knowledge, memory, and identity.

The West preserves its own while demanding we live inside theirs.

Even broken, fragments of our languages survived: codes when freedom was stolen, songs when chains were heavy, prayers when silence was forced. Language for us has never been decoration, it is survival, continuity, and divinity.

And yet, while our essence was stripped, the world pointed us toward something else: material comfort.

Beyond Material Comfort

Defenders of capitalism boast that the common person now lives better than kings of old, with cars, medicine, and electricity. But what they ignore is the cost: not in machines, but in memory.

For Black people, oppression was not only chains on the body but the stripping of culture and language. We were pushed to measure ourselves by their amenities, the house, the car, the wage, while our true inheritance was devalued.

But amenities are not essential. What we lost and must restore is deeper: our language, our culture, our ancestral way of divinity. It is there that we find frequency, alignment, and power as a people.

This is why language matters. It carries the rhythm of ancestors, the codes of survival, the pathways of spirit. To rebuild language is to resist erasure; to restore culture is to restore the self.

Ananse is not only a script. It is a law of clarity and a living operating system — threading us back to what amenities can never give: the memory of who we are, the vibration of what we carry, and the divinity of what we were never meant to lose.

Personalities Of Language-Soldier, Courtier, King, Seer, Etc.

The Personalities of Languages

Have you ever noticed that every language seems to carry a personality of its own? As if the way a people lived, fought, prayed, and dreamed soaked into their words until the language itself began to walk like a person? These are the patterns I've observed, and I ask you to look with me: do you see it too?

English ➜ The Soldier

Do you feel how English commands? Short, clipped, pragmatic. Almost militant. Could this be because it grew under conquest, empire, and law? English seems to march like a troop, swallowing words like spoils. Doesn't it sound like the voice of colonization itself?

French ➜ The Courtier

Does French not dress itself in elegance? Silent letters like jewels, accents like ornaments, preserved for prestige. Born in courts and diplomacy, French still feels like ceremony, charm, and seduction. Do you sense how it carries refinement more than necessity?

Arabic ➜ The King

When you hear Arabic, does it not feel majestic? Ordered, rhythmic. commanding reverence. Could it be that the Qur'an and classical poetry gave it this authority? Arabic curves like calligraphy on a crown, the voice of law and devotion.

Akan/Twi ➜ The Seer

Listen to Twi: Do you hear the proverb in every breath? It does not rush; it reveals. Could this be because Akan speech encodes memory in proverbs? Guiding generations like an elder? Doesn't it sound like the voice of ancestors, still speaking?

Chinese ➜ The Archivist

When you see Chinese characters, don't they feel like fossils alive? Each one is a keeper of history. Could it be that Chinese society's reverence for lineage and ancestors turned the language into an archive? Patient, disciplined, the guardian of memory.

Japanese ➜ The Artist

Do you notice the balance in Japanese? Kanji, Hiragana, Katakana - three scripts painting one canvas. Could it be that a culture of harmony and discipline shaped a language of brushstrokes, formal on one side, playful on the other?

Sanskrit ➜ The Sage

Do you hear in Sanskrit a vibration more than just words? Phonetics tied to breath, sound to cosmos. Wasn't it built by sages to mirror the order of the universe itself? Doesn't it feel like a meditating elder, reciting eternity?

Spanish ➜ The Dancer

When Spanish rolls off the tongue, doesn't it move like music? Upbeat, rhythmic, passionate. Could it be that those fiestas, songs, and empire expansion gave it this pulse? Spanish feels like a dancer in the plaza alive, inviting, irresistible. Do you feel that too?

German ➜ The Engineer

Do you notice how German builds? Compounding words like gears, precise, and forceful. Could its society's love for philosophy, law, and science have shaped this exactness? German feels like a builder of systems, structured, methodical, and solid.

Portuguese ➜ The Sailor-Poet

When the Portuguese speak, don't you hear waves? Rolling with longing, carrying saudade. Could it be that a seafaring people gave their tongue both melancholy and adventure? Doesn't it sound like a sailor-poet, writing on the horizon?

Swahili ➜ The Bridge

Do you notice that Swahili's rhythm is African at heart, yet layered? Within it live Portuguese, Persian, and Arabic. Could this be why it was promoted as the language for Africans in the diaspora? But ask yourself: is this truly the pure path back to self? Or does it point us sideways, to a bridge built by history's politics, instead of the deepest roots of our own?

Russian ➜ The Survivor

When Russian speaks, doesn't it feel heavy yet soulful? Forged in winters, wars, repression. Could this be why it carries both weight and song, hardship and soul (duša)? Russian seems like a survivor: wounded, enduring, but still singing deeply.

Africa: A Continent of Voices

If every language carries a personality, what about Africa, the continent with the greatest diversity of tongues on earth? Here, language is not just communication but drumbeat, proverb, chant, code. The personalities we mapped in English, French, Arabic, or Spanish don't we find them echoed, in even richer form, within African speech itself?

- The Soldier ➜ Isn't this the clipped, directive rhythm of Zulu commands, shaped in warrior tradition?
- The Courtier ➜ Do we not hear elegance in Wolof greetings, layered with formality and respect?
- The King ➜ Doesn't Amharic carry itself with majesty, like Ethiopia's throne that still honors its ancient script?
- The Seer ➜ Twi, Yoruba, and Igbo languages of proverbs, divination, and ancestral dialogue do they not embody the voice of prophecy?
- The Archivist ➜ Think of Ge'ez, still preserved in Ethiopian liturgy, or the inscriptions left in Nsibidi symbols. Guardians of memory.
- The Artist ➜ Shona and Xhosa, with clicks and tones woven like music, don't they paint sound itself into art?
- The Sage ➜ Ancient Egyptian (Medu Neter), Dogon cosmological terms, and Yoruba Ifá verses spiritual systems encoded in sound.
- The Dancer ➜ move like song Lingala, Kiswahili, and other Central African tongues roll and are vibrant, upbeat, calling bodies into rhythm.

- The Engineer ➜ Bantu languages with systematic noun classes, building order like architecture. Structure, precision, design.
- The Sailor ➜ Poet Fulani, Hausa, and other tongues that crossed the Sahara with trade, carrying longing, travel, poetry, and expansion. -
- The Bridge ➜ Kiswahili again, yes, hybrid absorbing foreign layers but always keeping the African drum at its core.
- The Survivor ➜ Don't we hear it in Creoles and Pidgins, born in oppression, carrying fragments of many tongues, yet still alive, still singing?

Africa is not missing from the map of language personalities it is the origin of the map. Every archetype we trace elsewhere exists here, often in its purest or earliest form.

Reflection

Language is not neutral. Do you see how it absorbs the life of its people, the battles they fought, the prayers they whispered, the ways they loved and governed? Over centuries, language begins to carry not just words but personality.

Europe and Asia show this, yes, but Africa sings it loudest, the continent where language dances, prophesies, commands, survives, and creates worlds.

So I ask you: pay attention to languages, especially African languages. See if you can map these personalities yourself. Notice how they reveal not just communication, but identity. I invite you: pay more attention to language.

Language Acquisition- Acquisition Vs Memorization

Language Acquisition

I know I have spoken much about the gift of Ananse how it restores clarity. how it reconnects us to memory, how it threads us back to ourselves. That truth is central. Yet alongside it, I also want to speak to those who carry another longing: the desire to gain a new tongue.

For many, language is not only survival, it is love. It is curiosity, passion, and the joy of stepping into another world. So let me offer this reflection not as rules, but as guidance. If you love languages, if you seek to acquire one, let it be done with reverence. Let it be done as an embrace of spirit, not just a chase for words.

How to Truly Learn a Language

Learning a language is not simply drills and memorization. To reduce it to lists and rules is to strip it of its essence. A language is not data; it is a living spirit. To learn it is not to conquer it, but to acquire it to step inside it until it begins to breathe through you.

Acquisition, Not Memorization

Memorization makes you repeat words. Acquisition makes you live them. True learning comes when you place yourself where you must use the language in conversations, in songs, in prayers, in laughter. The brain learns fastest when life is attached to the words.

The Culture is the Language

No language stands apart from its people. Their food, music, humor, and daily rhythm give breath to every syllable. To learn a language is to enter the home of its culture, to sit with its people, to taste how meaning is lived.

The Music of Speech

Every tongue has a rhythm. English marches. French flows. Spanish dances. Arabic recites. Twi prophesies. If you do not hear the tones, you will miss the spirit. Language is not only in what is said, but in the music beneath it, the rise, the fall, the pause, the silence.

Talking Drums-Tone as Law, African Science, Colonial Theft

The Talking Drum Beats

Before we cover tones, let me show you how vital tonality is. For Africans, tone was not ornament; it was law, so deep in secrecy and spirit that even drums could speak.

The Fascination of the Talking Drums

When you first hear the phrase talking drum, what conclusion do you reach? Do you imagine rhythm, spectacle, and dance as something exotic and distant? Or do you pause long enough to ask the deeper question: how can a drum truly talk?

This is where the mystery begins. For most, the thought of a drum that speaks feels strange, almost impossible. But for those who lived with it, there was nothing unusual at all. The talking drum was no novelty. It was spiritual technology, a science hidden in plain sight, a science later silenced, stolen, and nearly extinguished.

In its true form, the drum did more than create rhythm or stir a mood. It carried messages. Proverbs, praises, warnings, prayers, and even history itself traveled across distance through the pressure of an arm and the strike of a stick. Where European classical music refined harmony into emotion, the African talking drum refined language into rhythm. A violin may stir the heart, but a drum could declare a proverb that shaped the mind. A piano may evoke sorrow, but a drum could warn of danger drawing near. One cultivated feeling. The other transmitted meaning.

How Do Talking Drums Work?

The secret lies in tone. In Africa, the language itself is tonal pitch, meaning. The drum was designed with cords stretched along its body. By squeezing these cords beneath the arm, the drummer could tighten or loosen the skin, raising or lowering the pitch. Each strike imitated the rise and fall of the voice.

To outsiders, it may have sounded like rhythm or melody. To those who understood, it was intelligible speech. A skilled drummer could reproduce proverbs, greetings, names, prayers, and even conversations. Formulaic phrases or context clarified the message where needed, but the principle never changed: this was not folklore. This was linguistics woven into wood and hide. The drum was voice. The drum was law.

A comparison with European classical music

European classical traditions refined harmony, orchestration, and emotional landscapes. They made music a language of feeling. Yet the talking drum opened another path: the fusion of music with communication. Violin mood Drum message Orchestra emotion Drum ensemble = speech Both are profound, but only the talking drum shows that music does not need to stand beside language; it can be language.

Comparisons with World Tonal Systems

Tone is not unique to Africa. It is a universal law. In Mandarin, the syllable ma can mean "mother," "horse," "hemp," or "scold," depending only on pitch. In Twi, the word papa can mean "good," "father," or "fan," determined entirely by tone. Tone is not decoration. It is not melody draped on speech. It is the meaning itself. The talking drum made this visible, audible, and undeniable. Tone is law.

The High Science the World Lost

Imagine if the talking drum had been preserved and studied with the same reverence given to European instruments. Imagine if philosophers, scientists, and musicians had examined its laws as carefully as they examined harmony and notation.

The world, not only Africa, would be further today. Linguistics would have embraced tone as meaning centuries earlier. Communication technology might have evolved around pitch long before the invention of radio. Music would have been recognized as both emotion and logic, not torn into separate halves.

But prejudice stripped this science away. By branding Africa primitive, the colonizer locked away knowledge that belonged to all of humanity. Africa was robbed. But so too was the world.

Source Severed & Self-Extinguish

Appreciation for our source was taken away. We were taught to distrust our own wellspring until we stood with everything and nothing at the same time, equipped yet empty, present yet erased. Left like this long enough, a people begin to extinguish themselves, not for lack of genius but for lack of permission to honor it.

Tone, Diacritic-Placement + Curve = Sound + Sound

Rich in Linguistic

A people who could map speech into a drum, balancing tone with context, were not primitive. They were rich in linguistic genius.

We must ask: where did this mastery come from? How could those written off as "backward" hold such sophistication in both language and instrument? The truth is unsettling in its simplicity: what was dismissed as savagery was in fact a science too subtle to be measured by ink, paper, or colonial eyes.

To call it primitive was not ignorance. It was theft.

Fear of the Science

The drum was banned not because it was noisy, but because it was a signal. Power feared a science it did not understand, a tone-native relay of meaning that crossed distance without permission. What could not be decoded was outlawed. The fear was not of rhythm; it was of law carried in tone.

Envy, Trinkets, and Fracture

There was another theft more subtle, more corrosive. When drums were banned and tone suppressed, colonizers offered trinkets instead: small prizes, glittering distractions.

The trinket dazzled, and neighbors turned on neighbors. One flaunted the token, the other envied, both forgetting that the true wealth had already been stripped away. The bearer of the trinket was showcased as proof and often became the fool, paraded to validate the very system that emptied them. This is what I call negative individuality: the hunger to be seen with the prize, rather than to live as the source. A fractured value system, fed by envy and neediness. The drum might have bound them; instead, they were divided.

Children and the Musical Ear

Children raised in tonal systems in Africa, Asia, and beyond grew up hearing with different ears. Distinguishing high from low pitch was as natural as distinguishing cat from cut. Their training began in infancy. Language itself was a music practice.

This early attunement granted them sharper sensitivity to melody, intonation, and rhythm. While Western children often waited until choir or conservatory to shape their ears, these children were training every day through speech. This was not an accident. It was an inheritance. And with suppression of tone came suppression of this inheritance.

Al vs. African Drum Logic

Today, artificial intelligence can generate melodies, harmonies, and even lyrics. But to Al, a drum sound is only a sound. To Africans, that same sound was layered with meaning: A word, A warning, A praise, A proverb. Al manufactures emotion. The African drum delivered logic, law, and language. What the world dismissed as primitive was in truth a system of intelligence, a coded architecture of meaning through sound. A system alive long before artificial intelligence.

The Chilling Narrative of Replacement

Talk of mass extinction and the threat of AI can be chilling, more so when we imagine the possibilities with no moral law. Remember: tone already carries law. Where law is stripped of meaning, replacement narratives thrive. If we lose tone-as-law again, we lose the compass that tells the signal from the spectacle. By silencing the drum, humanity exiled its first native machine of intelligence. By forgetting tone, we risk exiling ourselves.

Tone as Soul and Spirit

Tone is not optional. Tone is the soul of speech. Without tone, language collapses into lifeless symbols.

The talking drum proved that tone is law: universal, binding, irreplaceable. The Ananse Stroke mirrors this law: One stroke, One law, Many revelations. Tone is sound and spirit. Tone is music and message. Tone is both feeling and logic. Ignore it, and you lose more than culture. You lose the thread of the soul itself.

Tones continued

Thus, we arrive at the Ananse Script. Here, tones are not ornaments or afterthoughts. They are the heart, the spirit, the bridge. A in plain form = mid tone, Stroke curved upward, high tone, Stroke flat, mid tone, Stroke curved downward = low tone

Placement curve sound + tone.

The same law that once allowed Africans to make drums speak now governs this script. The stroke is more than a mark: it is diacritic, it is law, it is bridge. Tones are not extras. They are what bind sound to meaning, and meaning to spirit.

Tones In the Ananse Script

Now for the tones, I didn't forget you at all. Yes, we left them for last, but that doesn't mean they're not important. If anything, that's their style. Tones are dramatic like that, always showing up fashionably late, but when they arrive, they change the whole vibe. They're the feeling gurus of language, pulling the strings of emotion and expression behind the scenes. Writing shows the body, but tone? Tone brings the soul.

Earlier, I reminded you that the first letter of each Ananse family must remain as it is without a stroke. That base form is the anchor of the system. Now we extend that rule to cover tones, but only for vowels. Some languages may place tones on consonants, but here, and for the Twi language in particular, we keep tones squarely on vowels.

The vowel A receives special treatment. Its base form, without any diacritic, represents the mid tone. When the Ananse stroke is added inside the shell, functioning as a diacritic, the tone changes:

-No diacritic (plain A) → diacritic) High tone Low tone Mid tone-Top inside stroke (Ananse stroke as Root inside stroke (Ananse stroke as diacritic) →Low tone

This gives A its full tonal range without clutter or extra marks. The other vowels (E, 1, O, U) follow the path we have already mentioned, and here's where it gets exciting. Their tones are not marked inside the shell-like A, but through the curved Ananse stroke acting as a diacritic:

Top curve (upward diacritic)→ High tone Flat stroke (no curve, diacritic) →Mid tone- Root curve (downward diacritic) ➝ Low tone

And that's it. Clean, clear, and expressive. No clutter of additional marks. The Ananse stroke itself works as the diacritic, carrying tone just as naturally as it carries family.

In the chapter "How the Stroke Works," I mentioned two main features of the Ananse stroke: its position and its curve. But in truth, there are at least two more. The stroke that transforms the vowel A is one of them, adding an extra vibe to the sound and giving it depth beyond the flat letter. This subtlety reveals the real genius of the stroke: it is not only a mark for sound, but also a sign that demystifies and empowers abstraction.

The stroke itself is more than a line on a page; it is an act. It represents the motion of pulling from abstract thought into the forefront of expression. It is like reaching into the unseen, into the cloud of possibilities, and dragging one clear shape into view. This is why the stroke feels alive.

It is not decoration, not clutter, not an afterthought. It is the very moment when silence becomes sound, when thought becomes symbol, when the hidden becomes shared. The Ananse Script does not just record language, it. Demonstrates how abstraction itself can be carried, revealed, and given form.

tones explained on twi word papa

Pàpá (low–high tone): Father

Pápá (high–high tone): Good

pàpà (low–low tone): Fan

The Ananse stroke with E

Let's focus our attention on how the Ananse Stroke shapes the word, Te.

There are no extra marks. It is always the same Ananse Stroke placed, then curved to carry tone.

The stroke always greets **E** at the top:

- If the stroke turns upward, it is still **E**, spoken high.
- If the stroke turns downward, it is still E, spoken low.

The same law flows into the other vowels:

- **I** is in the middle. Curve the stroke upward, and the sound rises high. Curve it downward, and the sound falls low.
- **O** rests at the root. Curve the stroke upward, and it rises. Curve it downward, and it sinks.

One stroke. One law.

Placement + curve = sound + tone.

Twi Tone Example

- **tè** (low tone) → to sit
- **té** (high tone) → to hear

Outro for vowel E

With this, we have seen how the Ananse Stroke works with the vowel **E**. The same law continues: the stroke placed at the top, middle, or root, curving up or down, carries tone without any extra marks.

The mid tone stands on its own, untouched, while the stroke does the rest.

One stroke. One law. The system remains simple and true.

And now, having walked through the families and vowels, it is time to test yourself on the journey so far.

Ntumpan- Great Drum as Voice of Kinship

Ntumpan (The Great Drum) & The Abusua

I couldn't resist mentioning the Ashanti abusua system and the talking drum. After all, one of the motives of this book is to familiarize readers with the rich African abusua tradition.

Among the Ashanti, the Ntumpan, the great talking drum, is not simply wood and skin. It is the voice of the abusua, the clan family. To hear it speak is to hear more than rhythm: it is to hear lineage, memory, and decree. Within the abusua, the drum affirms identity. Each family holds its rights and rhythms, its praises and proverbs, its subtle turns of tone that outsiders cannot always follow. The drum is not only music; it is a sign of belonging. When it sounds, it does not call all people equally. It calls its own. It is the clan's law beating in the air.

The Ntumpan speaks by bending the tone high, mid, and low, the very same pillars of the Twi language. This is not an accident. It is law; that tone carries meaning, and that meaning is guarded in the family.

How, then, might we join the Ntumpan to the Ananse Writing System? Both obey the same truth: tone is not extra, it is law. On the drum, cords are squeezed and released to lift or lower the voice. On the script, strokes curve upward, downward, or remain flat to mark tone. Both carry clan and spirit. The drum holds ancestral proverbs in sound, while the script holds ancestral wisdom in mark. The Ntumpan is the audible voice of the abusua, and the Ananse Script may be its silent counterpart, a written drum, a way to preserve what could be silenced but not erased.

MASTERY

Exam-Ananse Writing System (20 Question + Answer Key)

1. Why is the Ananse Stroke called the "Sound Organizer"?

2. What are the two main purposes of the Ananse Stroke?

3. Which sound is revealed when the stroke rests at the top of the Bilabial family?

4. Which sound appears when the stroke is placed in the middle of the Alveolars?

5. Which sound is uncovered when the stroke sits at the root of the Velars?

6. How many members are in the Alveolar family, and why is it one more than the Bilabials?

7. Why are the Velars described as the smallest family?

8. Which two sounds in the Bilabials are different, yet still belong to the family, and why?

9. Which two sounds in the Alveolars behave differently (one curls, one hisses)?

10. Why is Y unique among the Velars?

11. Why is H still included in the Velars, even though it behaves differently?

12. Why are vowels described as the open sounds of the system?

13. What happens when the stroke curves upward at the top of the vowel E?

14. What happens when the stroke curves downward at the middle of the vowel I?

15. What is the mnemonic phrase for the Bilabials?

16. What is the mnemonic phrase for the Velars?

17. What is the mnemonic phrase for the Vowels?

18. Which cultural principle are the Bilabials connected to?

19. Which cultural principle are the Alveolars connected to?

20. Which cultural principle are the Velars connected to?

Ananse Writing Answer Key

1. Because it keeps all sounds in order, revealing hidden members of families through placement and curve.

2. (a) To reveal the members of a family. (b) To show tone (high, mid, low).

3. B

4. T

5. K

6. Six members: N, D, T, L, R, S—one more than the Bilabials because of the unique sounds R and S.

7. They have only four members: G. K. H, Y.

8. F (breath between lip and teeth) and W (rounding the lips). They still belong because they are formed with the lips.

9. R (curls or flicks) and S (hisses).

10. Because it can act as both a vowel and a consonant.

11. Because it flows from the throat near the same region as the velar sounds.

12. Because they are formed with the mouth open and breath flowing freely.

13. It is spoken high.

14. It is spoken low.

15. Members: Be Prepared For Winning.

16. Greeting Kindly Honors You.

17. Air Energy In Our Universe.

18. Queen Mother nurture, continuity, inheritance.

19. Kingship rule, order, authority.

20. Priesthood wisdom, guidance, bridging heaven and earth.

Postscript Beyond the Basics

What has been shown so far is only the foundation of the Ananse Script. Four shells, one stroke, three placements this is the starting point, the doorway. But the system does not end here.

The Ananse Script grows.

It reaches outward into the Akan family tree, where letters are not only sounds but lineages, carrying the rhythm of inheritance and kinship. It reaches deeper into African cosmology, where shells are tied to creation, spirit, and ancestral order. It shapes itself through letter. omissions, teaching that silence is also part of sound. It extends into code writing, where the same rules guide abstraction, encryption, and hidden design.

The rules remain simple. Once the learner understands the four shells and the rhythm of placement, the rest can unfold without limit. The shell is only a container and containers can change.

If one shell is replaced, it does not break the system. The meaning continues. The Ananse Script is not bound to form, but to principle. It is the builder of letters, the carrier of meaning.

Punctuation and numbers are also part of the system. In Ananse, the end of a sentence is marked by writing the last letter in capital form. The final capital represents the full stop. Its spiritual teaching is that the beginning and the end are one.

There are many books about the Abusua family on Scribd and other platforms for those who wish to explore further.

The basics open the door. What comes after is an entire horizon.

From Language to Spirit - Writing as Shrine and Memory

What we have studied so far shows that the Ananse Writing System is more than a tool for spelling words. It is a vessel of order, of memory, of clarity. People who master their script master their reflection; they no longer borrow another's mirror to see themselves.

But writing is not only about sounds and signs. It is also about how we live, how we build, and how we clothe the sacred. A script that carries memory can also carry dignity. A stroke that organizes sound can also organize spirit.

As we turn now to belief and aesthetics, remember this: the Ananse Script is not simply for paper, it is for shrines, for monuments, for the spaces where we meet God and Ancestors. Where there was neglect, it brings beauty. Where there was silence, it inscribes memory. Where there was bare ground, it clothed faith with honor.

Twi Language Depth - Ka & Ba, Continuity & Spirit

Twi, the living tongue of the Akan, is more than a medium of communication; it carries proverbs, history, and ancestral worldview in every utterance. Linguistically, Twi sits within the Akan dialect continuum of the Kwa branch in the Niger-Congo family. In Twi, words rarely stand alone; one syllable can branch into many meanings, and **context** decides which branch carries the truth.

Location & Speakers. Twi is spoken primarily in southern and central Ghana and across parts of Côte d'Ivoire. Within Ghana, Akan (the wider cluster that includes Twi and Fante) functions as a lingua franca across markets, churches, media, and governance. Estimates vary by source, but a reasonable picture is this: Twi has an estimated **8-10 million native speakers,** with many more using it fluently as a second language across Ghana and the wider Akan diaspora.

Twi holds ancient wisdom in living form. Its proverbs, its way of naming, and its spiritual vocabulary-words like okra (soul), sunsum (spirit), and abosom (deities)- show that philosophy is embedded in everyday talk.

In my study of Twi, I focused on two small but powerful words: ka and ba.

- ka means to say, to tell, to resemble, to add, to owe, and even to bite or strike. At its heart lies **expression, likeness, attachment.**
- ba means to come, to return, a child, a descendant. At its heart. lies, **arrival, continuity, and generational presence.**

What I came to realize is that these words echo spiritual concepts once carried in **Kemet (ancient Egypt).** The resemblance is not shallow but rooted in meaning: ka tied to life force and likeness; ba tied to soul, movement, and return. Though millennia stand between them, I hold no doubt of the linkage. This conviction rests not only on what I have read or heard, but also on my own research and my visits: in **West Africa**, through the speech I heard; and in **Egypt,** through the walls and what the Ancients left engraved for us to see.

For this reason, we should search across African languages for such fragments. Even in the simplest syllables, we may find residues of ancient spiritual systems-carried forward, hidden in plain sight, awaiting recognition.

When I reflect on the speech habits of Black communities across the West Indies and America, I see how often context has been stripped away. Words are used in flat, generalized ways, leaving behind only the surface. Someone may be called "great" or "strong," but without context, what is meant? Is the greatness in **basketball, football, music, art, service, or moral standing**? Is the strength of the body or of the spirit? Without context, the word floats.

This loss is not because our people lack depth, but because we were **cut from our speech.** The ancestral habit of grounding words in a proverb and context was broken, leaving behind conversation that can feel still less insightful than it should be.

To restore context is to restore depth. It places words back in their rightful soil and allows them to breathe again. And it is this principle that now prepares the way for the **Ananse Stroke**, where the mark itself will reveal what our speech has always known: context is never extra, but everything.

Manifesto 1- A Cry for Grounding

Abusua is the sacred family system that binds ancestry, blood, and responsibility into one covenant. Ifá the Yoruba system of divination, where wisdom is carried through signs, verses, and stories linking the seen with the unseen. These remind us that the script is not decoration; it is spirit.

Africans have not yet uplifted Africa's spirit in a way that truly belongs to us. Modernization is too often defined for us, not by us. A few leaders strive to turn us back toward our ground, Ibrahim Traoré with his defiance, Julius Malema with his fire, and Professor Lumumba with his clarity. Yet as a people, we remain unawakened to our full capacity. The journey is unfinished, a work still in progress. The family systems and sacred beliefs that once held us upright remain buried beneath borrowed letters and foreign tongues. We write with marks not ours, shaping our thoughts into molds never meant for us.

Look at the world: Japan endured nuclear fire, yet still writes in the strokes of its ancestors. China bore humiliation, yet its script endures. India was broken open, yet her chants in script survive. The Middle East is torn apart, yet Arabic binds its people. The First Nations of the Americas, though scattered, still fight to breathe life into their tongues. And Africa? We remain broken not only by chains, but by the severing of script, the cutting off of letters, the breaking of spirit.

Even today, in 2025, I see the signs: school walls demanding "Speak English only. Speak French only." Children are shaped to forget before they can remember. We, who once held scripts of our own, are told to abandon them. We are forced to adapt, and in that adaptation, we lose sight of ourselves. Writing was once our mirror, always in rhythm with our people.

Every culture honors its ancestors. Europe cloaks cities with symbols. Rome crowns government halls with carved emblems. Old Saxon and Viking names, forced into our mouths, now sound normal because force made them normal. Our surnames, Braithwaite, Robinson, Johnson, Smith, and Williams, are signatures of ownership where Abusua names once stood. They branded us until we spoke them as though they belonged to us. And still, Jews across the world, whether you call them true or not, strive for unity, while Africans scorn what is theirs and embrace what was beaten and forced into them.

But Africa has never been without voices who tried to restore its script. Scholars and inventors across West Africa carried the struggle forward: Souleymane Kanté, who gave the Manding languages the N'Ko script. Momolu Duwalu Bukele, who created the Vai syllabary in Liberia. Fallou Ngom, who documented Ajami manuscripts written in Arabic script. David Roberts and John Victor Singler studied tone, orthography, and the challenges of representing sound across scripts.

Each of these efforts carried the same spirit: African sounds deserve African order. Some borrowed Arabic or Latin letters, others built new systems, but all sought to return rhythm and dignity to our languages.

The Ananse Script stands in that same lineage. It continues their vision, but with a different path: four shells, one stroke, and the organization of sound families already alive in Twi and across Africa.

Yet you, reader, are here. That alone is proof that the awakening has already begun. You did not stumble into these words by accident; you were called. To take this journey is to take part in healing a wound that has lingered for centuries. By reading, remembering, and reclaiming, you join the work of lifting Africa's spirit not as an abstraction, but as a living ground beneath our feet.

But mourning alone is not enough. To reclaim is not only to look back, but to move forward. What Africa needs is not only memory, but clarity, a vision simple enough for the child, strong enough for the people, and clear enough to guide us into tomorrow. This is the work of the Ananse Script.

Manifesto 2 - A Call for Healing

Too often, in our communities, it is neighbor against neighbor, brother against brother, cousins against cousins, all over the most nonsensical things. We turn our frustration inward, and instead of building, we break even more.

Too often, we have traded the strength of the family for the weakness of individuality. The ancients knew what we have forgotten: strength was never in the lone man, but in the circle, in the family, in the community that holds him upright.

When I say reparations through policy, I do not mean only a hope for checks or financial compensation. Black people rightly want material redress, but money alone will not undo the chains. Policies are the modern-day ships and chains of institutions that carry advantage and oppression. We must study the associations of the past and recognize that slave ships today are policies that oppress us. Reparations must be structural, not cosmetic: laws and systems changed so they no longer reproduce the harms of yesterday.

Policies that continue to oppress the American prison system, foster care pipelines, broken homes, and institutional neglect remain operative and lethal. They must be overturned.

Too often, many African Americans show no regard for Africa and see Mother as a mockery. This is the negativity of individuality at its strongest. Yet in my travels, I have seen otherwise: in India, where ancestors are remembered daily, memory keeps the living connected to the dead, and through that, to life itself.

Today, it seems as if Africans no longer truly own Africa, with the weight of exploitation by foreign powers stripping resources, land, and dignity. But ownership is more than resources; it is spirit, culture, and law rooted in our people.

And yet another wound remains: too often, Africans in Africa stretch their hands to receive from the brothers and sisters who return, while holding inside a feeling that they are somehow different from them. This divide must be brought into account. Leaders of African countries must not only ask us to rally to their cause, but also teach their people to feel the pain of those who were sold, and to make amends.

Even in visiting the castles where our foreparents were held, we are asked to pay while natives enter freely. I myself always jump the fence, because the portal is still intact, the place they call the "Door of No Return." It should have been transformed into a symbol of Sankofa love, a doorway of healing. Instead, it remains exactly as the Europeans left it, while African leaders keep it as a cash cow, not a well of reconciliation. This shows no sign of true compensation, no rebuilding with honest effort, no demonstration of love that heals.

The Ananse Writing System is ours our own script, born of our breath and organs, our family of sounds. It is not borrowed, it is not imposed. It is our memory returned to us, and it can assist in bridging the gap between those who remained and those who return. With it, we write ourselves whole again, and we stand on ground that belongs to us.

Africa must be rebuilt, not on what money can buy. It needs its spiritual way of life restored, built to rival religion itself, and the wisdom is already there. Our wealth is in spirit, in culture, in law and song, in the wisdom of ancestors.

When she rises, she must not rise to oppress. She must not rise to impress. She must rise to protect. Africa needs its own leadership, its own haven, not just for Africans, but for the return of uprightness among men.

This is our Exodus. Africans near and far must rally for unity, not expecting one man or woman to lead the way. The family system is our foundation, the script is our memory, and the sound is our healing.

At first, I almost left AI out as if forgetting to name the shadow already shaping our lives. But it cannot be ignored. AI is an extension of our reach and our thought, and so it must be treated with care. Humans can rival it not by trying to beat it in its own code, but by living beside it with spiritual intelligence. Used well, AI becomes a mirror and a lever- an extension that helps us re-tune our minds and rebuild balance, rather than erase our memory. We cannot afford to let AI become another master. It must remain a servant, a regulator, a helper to return us to ourselves.

Manifesto 3 - True Worship Vs Neglect

In our modern lives, Africans chase the aesthetics of the West: tiled floors, polished gadgets, shiny cars, and the allure of luxury. Yet when it comes to the spaces of our God, the very ground of Mother Earth, we leave them bare, harsh, and neglected. What does it mean that the place where we pray looks stripped of beauty, while the place where we consume is dressed in style?

Just as we treat the land, so we treat our beliefs. When shrines look derogatory and uninviting, it is not because our faith is weak; it is because we have not clothed it with pride.

Honor is simple. It avoids the trap of lavish worship, of money-hoarding temples, of chasing luxury in the name of spirit. Honor means balance, dignity, and beauty that welcome both people and God. Our shrines and monuments should now carry the Ananse Script, marking them with our own writing and memory, not borrowed tongues.

And let it be clear, when we speak of the "gods" of Africa, we do not mean rival deities. We mean the energies (forces of nature, guardians of elements, ancestral powers) that flow from the One Supreme God. This is not polytheism, but harmony energies honored as living expressions of the Source.

Compare the two: one scene shows worship marked by harshness and decay, the other shows worship uplifted, cared for, inscribed, and alive with aesthetics. Which one draws the spirit closer? Which one tells the world that our belief system is worthy of reverence.

Respect Overdue - Shrines and Sacred Spaces

Respect overdue

Final Exam- Comprehensive Review

Final Mastery Test - The Ananse Writing System

Instruction: Circle or mark the correct answer. Read carefully; some questions test meaning beneath the surface.

1.　What does the Ananse Stroke represent at its core?

A. The voice of Europe's alphabet

B. A thread connecting sound, family, and meaning

C. A silent mark of punctuation

D. A tonal accent is only used for vowels

2. How many shells form the base of the Ananse system?

A. 3

B. 4

C. 5

D. 6

3. Which statement best describes "collapse into 4"?

A. Reducing letters to four syllables of Latin

B. Simplifying English spelling rules

C. Condensing all sounds into four ancestral groups

D. Removing tone from writing

4. The placement of a stroke (top, mid, root) determines:

A. Color of ink

B. Meaning

C. Tone and family relation

D. Font size

5. Which of the following is not one of the four sound families?

A. Bilabials

B. Alveolars

C. Velars

D. Nasals

6. Bilabials are symbolically linked with:

A. The King

B. The Priest

C. The Queen Mother

D. The People

7. Mnemonic for Bilabials ("Members Be Prepared For Winning") reminds us that:

A. Speech begins with open lips

B. Every family has five members

C. Lips give life through nourishment and breath

D. Words are tools of warfare

8. The Alveolar family is associated with:

A. Authority and law

B. Emotion

C. Wind

D. Silence

9. Velars (GKHY) represent:

A. The Priesthood

B. The Farmer

C. The Child

D. The Trader

10. The Vowel family stands for:

A. Healers

B. The People

C. The Animals

D. The Winds

11. In the Ananse Script, tone is controlled by:

A. Color changes

B. Stroke curve and placement

C. Capital letters

D. Spacing

12. How many primary tone levels are recognized?

A. 2

B. 3

C. 4

D. 5

13. The Twi word papa changes meaning through:

A. Tone variation

B. Extra letters

C. Suffix marks

D. Repetition

14. Talking drums communicate by:

A. Drum size only

B. Pitch patterns matching speech tones

C. Random rhythm

D. Lyrics engraved on skin

15. Tone, in African science, is understood as:

A. Decoration

B. Energy Law

C. Volume control

D. Musical entertainment

16. Abusua represents:

A. A single sound

B. A clan or lineage system

C. A drum pattern

D. A set of tones

17. Which comparison captures Ananse vs. English logic?

A. English adds letters: Ananse reveals relations

B. English removes tone; Ananse ignores sound

C. Both depend on spelling memory only.

D. Ananse uses 26 letters like English

18. When applied to quantum computing, the four shells symbolize:

A. Binary digits

B. Quantum states in superposition

C. Computer fonts

D. Keyboard keys

19. Privacy in Ananse Script is described as:

A. Secrecy against truth

B. Freedom through personal cipher

C. Isolation from others.

D. Encryption for machines only

20. The title "Sound Weaver" means:

A. One who memorizes rules

B. One who connects spirit, language, and creation through sound

C. A drummer only

D. A scribe without voice

Final Mastery Test Answer Key

1) B

2) B

3) C

4) C

5) D

6) C

7) C

8) A

9) A

10) B

11) B

12) B

13) A

14) B

15) B

16) B

17) A

18) B

19) B

20) B

Scoring Guide

17-20 correct → Master of Sound & Symbol

13-16 correct → Ananse Apprentice

9-12 correct → Sound Traveler

Below 9 → Return to the Drum and Listen Again

Afterword - Exodus, Unity and Spirit Restored

What you hold in your hands is not merely a book; it is a reminder that our story has never ended. Across centuries of interruption, our memory was forced underground, but like roots beneath stone, it kept growing.

The Ananse stroke, the four-letter alphabet, the echoes of our tongues, these are not inventions of today, but awakenings. They call us back to a rhythm older than conquest and sharper than erasure. In every mark, in every sound, we hear the voice of those who came before, whispering: continue.

I did not write these pages to close a chapter, but to open a door. Language is not just a tool for speaking; it is the bridge between spirit and survival, between ancestors and descendants. If these words have touched you, then the work is already alive in you.

Take what you have learned here and carry it into your homes, your schools, your prayers, and your technologies. Let the revival of our tongues and symbols move like fire through a dry field. For as long as we breathe, no reset can silence us.

This is not the end, it is a continuation. The ink is yours now.

REFERENCE AND END MATTER

Definition And Disclaimer

Sound Arrangement

- This system arranges sounds by where they happen in the mouth.
- Some names may look different from how they appear on the IPA (International Phonetic Alphabet) chart.
- IPA uses older categories; here, we follow the movement and starting point of the sound.

Vowels (Open Sounds / Breath)

Let's get vowels out of the way first since they're the easiest.

- In Akan Twi, there are seven vowel sounds.
- For clarity, this book uses only the five vowels common in English: A, E, I, O, U.
- This means that instead of the full 22 Akan sounds, we will be discussing 20 sounds in this book.

Now, here come the big linguistic jargons I mentioned before. Don't worry, every time you see one of those heavy names, I'll guide you with parentheses so you know their basic meaning right away.

Consonant Families

- Bilabial (2 Lips): M, B, P, F, W
- Note: Linguists often call F a labio-dental (lip + teeth).

- Note: Linguists often call W a semi-vowel (half vowel, half consonant).
- In this system, both remain bilabial lips are the main tool.

Alveolar (Ridge Behind Teeth): N, D, T, L, R, S

- S: often called an alveolar fricative (air pushed along the ridge).
- R: often called an alveolar approximant (tongue close but not fully touching).
- In this system, both the alveolar tongue + ridge remain the anchor.

Velar (Back of Mouth / Soft Palate): K, G, H, Y

- Y: linguists often label as palatal (tongue rising higher toward the back).
- Here, it rises from the same space as velar sounds, so it remains velar.

Tone: The Music of Sound

Sound in Africa is not only where the tongue, lips, or throat meet. It is also in the music, the tone.

Core levels:

- High (↑)
- Mid/Flat (→)
- Low (↓)

Examples of more complex tone behaviors (seen in languages like Yoruba, Igbo, Chinese):

- Contour tones:
- Rising
- Falling
- Falling— Rising
- Rising-— Falling

- Down step (↓H): a high tone slightly lower than the one before (like a staircase).
- Up step (↑H): a high tone raised above normal.
- Tone sandhi: tones that change depending on neighboring tones.
- Floating tones: tones without their own vowel, attaching to the next syllable.
- Tone spreading/terracing: tones step down or stretch across a phrase.

Important Note for the Reader: Do not get confused. These examples are shown only to help you see how tone can work across different languages. In this book, we are only dealing with three tones: High, Mid/Flat, and Low.

The beauty of the Ananse Stroke is that it does not need extra marks:

- Curve up =High tone
- Flat =Mid tone
- Curve down =Low tone

That is elegant because:

- The stroke's position shows the family.
- The stroke's curve shows the tone.
- One mark does both jobs — no clutter, no extra signs.

Note on Redundancy and Scope

Some of this may feel repeated, and that's intentional. Repetition is not confusion; it is reinforcement. The same mouth movement often explains more than one sound.

By the end of this book, the system will be clear and uncluttered. You don't need digraphs (two-letter combos). For deeper study, you can explore a comprehensive Twi book or a Twi phrasebook.

There is no equivalent of the English apostrophe + s ('s) in Twi. The relationship is clear from the syntax, the order of words and particles.

Twi comprehensive

Twi phrase book

Added Guidance for the Reader

To help you digest these ideas without feeling forced, I have placed questions and answers after each major section. These are not tests; they are gentle pauses, a chance to reflect, to see what has settled, and to engage without pressure.

From time to time, you will also notice a touch of humor woven into the pages. This is not to take away from the seriousness of the subject, but to keep the rhythm of learning light. Our ancestors understood that wisdom can be carried both by solemn words and by playful trickster tales.

And just like those tales, you will meet Ananse himself throughout these pages, sometimes as art, sometimes with a word of encouragement. He will remind you, in his way, that every web is built strand by strand, and learning is no different.

Glossary Of Linguistic Terms

Tone - The pitch of your voice (high, mid, low) that can change the meaning of a word.

Contour Tone - A tone that changes within one syllable (example: starts low then rises).

Downstep - A high tone that is a little lower than the previous high tone, like stepping down stairs.

Upstep - A high tone that is a little higher than the previous high tone, like stepping up stairs.

Tone Sandhi - When the tone of a word changes because of the word before or after it. Floating Tone - A tone with no sound of its own that attaches to the next syllable.

Tone Spreading/Terracing - When a tone stretches over several words or steps down gradually like a staircase.

Digraph - Two letters that work together to make one sound (example: sh in ship). Syntax: The structure and order of words in a sentence.

Possession - How a language shows ownership (English uses 's, Twi shows it through word order).

Jargon - Technical or expert language that feels complicated for everyday people.

Homonym - Words that sound the same or are spelled the same but have different meanings (bat = animal or baseball stick).

Homograph - Words spelled the same but with different meanings and sometimes different pronunciations (lead metal vs. lead to guide).

Homophone - Words that sound the same but are spelled differently and mean different things (two, to, too).

Orthography - The writing system of a language (letters, spelling, and writing rules).

Redundancy - Repetition built into a system. In language, it means repeating information to make things clearer or easier to remember.

Minimal Pair - Two words that differ by only one sound, showing how a single sound can change meaning (pat vs. bat).

References

A

- Akan (see also Twi), pp. 7–8
- Ananse, gift of, pp. 29–36
- Ananse stroke (writing system), pp. 29–36
- Ancestral memory/presence, pp. 65–67, 127–134
- Anthropocene, pp. 1–2
- Artificial intelligence (AI), pp. 82–91
- Alphabet, four-letter, pp. 11–21, 29–31
- African languages, pp. 8–10, 93–100
- African scholars, pp. 93–96

B

- Bibliography, pp. 159

C

- Christaller, pp. 159
- Code (programming), pp. 82–91
- Colonial exploitation, pp. 1–3
- Cultural acceleration, pp. 1–2

E

- English vs. African languages, pp. 7–9
- English alphabet vs. new script, pp. 7–11
- Erasure/renaming, pp. 2–3
- Europe exploitation, pp. 1–2

- Echoes/Vibration wording, pp. 1–2

F

- Family system, pp. 29–31, 65–67
- Flow of philosophy/science, pp. 1–2
- Frequency of another age, pp. 1–2
- Four-letter alphabet, pp. 11–12, 29

G

- Gold trade, pp. 1–2

H

- Historians' view, pp. 1–2
- History interruptions, pp. 1–2

I

- Immersion vs memorization, pp. 114
- Indian linguistic method, pp. 9–11
- Invocation, pp. 15–16
- Isolation of West Africa, pp. 1–2

K

- Kwadwo, Nana, pp. 65

L

- Language acquisition (tones), pp. 114–119
- Language as survival, pp. 1–2, 133–136
- Letters vs sounds, pp. 7–8
- Linguistics (general), pp. 93–100

M

- Manifesto, pp. 136–142
- Memorization vs acquisition, pp. 114
- Minimal pairs, pp. 9–10
- Memory as temple of sound, pp. 1–2
- Modern global OS, pp. 82–91

N

- Names changed, pp. 2–3
- North/Northeast Africa, pp. 1–2

O

- Oppression, pp. 1–3
- Operating system global, pp. 82–91

P

- Panini, pp. 9–10
- Prologue, pp. 1–16
- Proof inside languages, pp. 7–10

R

- References, pp. 159
- Reset (historical/cultural), pp. 1–3
- Revival of tongues, pp. 8–10, 133–136

S

- Sahara as wall, pp. 1–2
- Sankofa, pp. 65

- Scholars (African), pp. 93–96
- Script (new writing system), pp. 29–36
- Ships (European), pp. 1–2
- Sounds vs letters, pp. 7–8
- Spirit vs letters, pp. 1–2
- Survival through language, pp. 1–2

T

- Temple of sound, pp. 1–2
- Twi, pp. 8–9

U

- Upliftment, pp. 133–136

V

- Vibration of change, pp. 1–2
- Variety & memorization, pp. 70–71

W

- West Africa (isolation/flows), pp. 1–2
- Writing system, pp. 29–36

IPA

THE INTERNATIONAL PHONETIC ALPHABET

CONSONANTS (PULMONIC)

	Bilabial	Labiodental	Dental	Alveolar	Postabverolar	Retoflex	Velar	Uvular	Glottal
Plosive	p	b	t	r		ŋ	q	x	q
Nasal	n	n	—	r	r	ɽ	v		
Trill	f		v						w
Fricative	f f ʋ	f h j	ʒ l z	ṙ ɽ		x	ɣ	ɑ	l
Lateral appross	1	1	1		ɟ	1			
Approv ??onant	1			l	l				

Symbols to night in a axell, the 'left tior oood." Shaded areas indicate atticulationes ipossible,

CONSONANTS (NON-PULMONIC)

Clicks	Voiced implosives	Ejectives
W Bilabial	q Billdiial	ʌ Alveolar
d Dental	ɗ DentalAiveotar	y Velar
p) (Postialves)	ʎ Palatal	ʯ Uvular
a Alveolar	x Velar	

OTHER SYMBOLS

- W Voiceless labial-velar fric
- y Voiced labial-palatal
- z̄ Voied cipgillatal
- s Mid centraal vovel
- ɰ Alvoolo-patiat fricative
- ɸ Epiglorial plosive
- 3 Epigrezed plosive
- Tn respecitionse

DIACRITICS

Voiceless	ɦ	Voiced '	ə	Apiral
Voiced	ṯ	Aspirated	'h	l In X
More rounded	O	Less rounded	#	Contralizzied
Advanced	⊥	Retracted	=	Mid
Syllabic	ɞ	Nasalized	ʃ	Nasalisalizd
Rhoticity	=	—	b	Denasalized
Some	ɦ	Sano sysi.	B	—

Some diacrities may be piaceel above a syibol with descenders c̄.

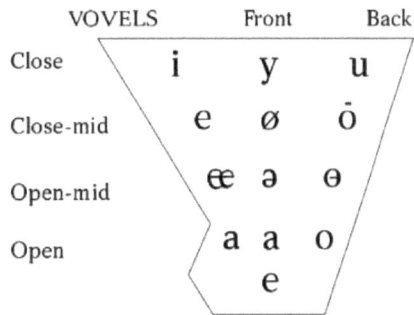

VOVELS

	Front		Back
Close	i	y	u
Close-mid	e	ø	ō
Open-mid	ɶ	ə	ɵ
Open	a a		o
	e		

tʃ dȝ

SUPRASEGMENTALS

- Primary stress
- Secondary stress
- Long
- Half-long
- Minor (foot)
- Major (intonaton)
- Syllable break
- Linking

SUPRASEGMENTALS

- LEVEL
- Primary stress
- Long
- Half-long

www.ingramcontent.com/pod-product-compliance
Lightning Source LLC
Chambersburg PA
CBHW060812010526
44117CB00002B/16